John Robert Seeley

A Short History of Napoleon the First

Vol. 1

John Robert Seeley

A Short History of Napoleon the First
Vol. 1

ISBN/EAN: 9783337350475

Printed in Europe, USA, Canada, Australia, Japan

Cover: Foto ©ninafisch / pixelio.de

More available books at **www.hansebooks.com**

A SHORT HISTORY

OF

NAPOLEON THE FIRST.

BY

JOHN ROBERT SEELEY,

REGIUS PROFESSOR OF MODERN HISTORY IN THE UNIVERSITY OF CAMBRIDGE, AND AUTHOR OF "ECCE HOMO," ETC.

With a Portrait.

BOSTON:
ROBERTS BROTHERS.
1886.

PREFACE.

To write a life of Napoleon which shall be positively short is not possible. When I undertook to write one in twelve pages of the 'Encyclopædia Britannica,' I thought I was attempting what was difficult; but I was mistaken; I was attempting what was impossible. I take this opportunity of acknowledging the liberality of the Messrs. Black, who, in compliance with my wishes, and, I believe, at considerable inconvenience to the arrangements of the Encyclopædia, actually allowed me thirty-six pages, or not less than three times the space which had been originally allotted for the article. The same publishers now place me under another obligation in consenting to smooth my way to the present 'Short History,' in which the substance of that article is incorporated.

The Life of Napoleon now given to the public is, if not absolutely short, yet, measured by the space allotted in it to each incident, almost as short as the obituary notice of a newspaper. It dismisses more than one great campaign with a sentence, more than one famous battle with a line. In the Encyclopædia this was unavoidable, but the reader may ask whether there can be any justification for issuing as a book a summary which must needs, he may think, be as jejune as a table of contents.

I admit at once that for some purposes this Short History of Napoleon must be wholly useless, but I flatter myself that for certain other purposes it may be all the more satisfactory for being so exceedingly brief. A bewilderment caused by the multitude of facts and details is the danger which chiefly besets the reader of history; and where, as in Napoleon's career, facts are unusually crowded together, the danger is greatest, the bewilderment most overwhelming. I have held it possible to meet this difficulty by almost suppressing details, and thus diminishing to the utmost the demand made upon the attention and memory, but at the same time to atone for what is lost in coloring and light and shadow by clearness of outline.

Nothing certainly could be more lifeless than a mere chronological catalogue of Napoleon's achievements; but I thought that a narrative almost as brief as a catalogue would not be uninteresting, and still less useless, if it successfully brought together cause and effect, traced development clearly, and showed convincingly the influence of the age upon the man, and of the man upon his age.

Preface.

I have, therefore, subordinated everything to clearness and unity, and there are some aspects of the life which, to gain room, I have consciously omitted altogether. For instance, no attempt is made here either to describe or to estimate Napoleon as a military commander. I do not write a soldier's history of him, and accordingly, though I endeavor to give the strategical outline of each campaign correctly, the battles will be found to be not only not described, but not even narrated; they are merely registered. Again, I refrain almost entirely from drawing upon the fund of private, personal, or domestic detail and anecdote, though it is upon matter of this kind that a biography commonly depends for its vividness. The Duchess of Abrantès, Bourrienne, Mme. de Rémusat, and many similar writers less well known, stood ready to supply such matter in no small quantity; but I wished my narrative to be clear and short, and comparatively I cared little that it should be vivid.

I thought such a plan feasible, but I did not flatter myself that it would be easy. It is particularly difficult to gain a comprehensive view of those historical persons who have an international position. Napoleon is a leading figure in the domestic history of every great continental state, and the greatest foreign enemy in the history of England, yet most of his historians have regarded him almost exclusively from the point of view of a single state. They have written as Frenchmen or as Englishmen, not only with limited sympathies, but actually for the most part with most imperfect knowledge.

Such an outline as I meditated, at once short and trustworthy, could not be produced by mere compilation from ordinary authors, or by hasty investigations. I must ask the reader to believe that I have not studied Napoleon's life in order to write this little book, but that I write the book because I have for years studied the Napoleonic age from many points of view, and in many countries. I need not ask him to take this entirely on credit. I have shown in my 'Life and Times of Stein' (1879) that I have investigated thoroughly the revolutions produced by the Napoleonic wars in Germany. From my 'Expansion of England' (1883) he may satisfy himself that I have reflected on the relations of France and England in the Napoleonic age, and on the gradual growth throughout the eighteenth century of that quarrel between the two nations which reached such a height under Napoleon. But since the publication of that book and during the composition of this, I have pursued those inquiries further, being engaged upon a 'History of English Foreign Policy during the Eighteenth Century.' And I draw my information at first hand from the manuscript despatches preserved at the Record Office.

Preface. vii

As to the French aspect of the subject, I have endeavored here too to rest as much as possible upon documents. My chief study has lain, not in Thiers or Lanfrey, but in the Napoleon Correspondence. I may add that my view of the connection of Napoleon with the Revolution, and of the development of the Napoleonic out of the Revolutionary age, is the result of much study of the latter as well as of the former.

Beside original documents I have of course studied the works founded on original documents which have appeared of late years. Among the recently opened sources to which this volume is indebted, I would mention particularly, on the earlier period, Jung's works; on the period of the Directory, Hüffer's, the later volumes of Von Sybel, and the study on the Egyptian expedition by Count Boulay de la Meurthe; on the German wars, the genuine memoirs of Hardenberg, edited by Ranke, and Ranke's biography of him, Oncken on the 'War of Liberation,' and a long list of books already used by me in the 'Life and Times of Stein.' But some important works have appeared since that publication, especially the second volume of Oncken, and Treitschke's history; I may also mention the original researches which are now being made by A. Stern.

Almost one-third of this volume is occupied by an essay on Napoleon, which is entirely new. It is designed to correspond with the History to which it is appended, and makes use of no materials but such as are furnished by the History. It could not therefore attempt either to analyze his character or estimate his genius. The question it deals with is rather his relation to his age, his place in the history of France and of Europe, and even on this question — I need hardly say — it offers only suggestions. It is only an essay; it is not a treatise.

Our portrait is from an engraving after a picture by Boilly, which represents Napoleon as First Consul, and bears date 29 Thermidor, an X. It was executed in mezzotint, and several impressions of it, all alike colored by hand (it is doubtful whether any uncolored impressions were published), are preserved in the Bibliothèque Nationale at Paris. We give the head; but in the original, which is on a considerably larger scale than our copy, the portrait is enclosed in an oval frame, below which is engraved a review in the Place du Carrousel, with the inscription 'Révue du Quintidi.'

The cast of the face of Napoleon was taken in wax on the morning after his death. It was brought to England in 1855, and was excellently engraved in the 'Illustrated London News.' We are indebted to the proprietor for permission to reproduce the wood-cuts.

CONTENTS.

CHAPTER I.

BUONAPARTE.

§ 1. Buonaparte's Birth and Family. — Military Education. — Early Authorship 9
§ 2. Corsican Period 15
§ 3. At Toulon. — Joins the Army of Italy. — Connection with the Robespierres. — Ordered to the Army of the West. — Remains in Paris . 23
§ 4. Checks Revolt of the Sections. — Marriage. — Commander of the Army of Italy 32

CHAPTER II.

GENERAL BONAPARTE.

§ 1. Italian Campaign 37
§ 2. Acts as Independent Conqueror. — Levying of Contributions. — His Italian Policy. — Advance on Austria. — Preliminaries of Leoben. — Occupation of Venice. — Fructidor. — Treaty of Campo Formio 43
§ 3. The Revolution of Fructidor 57
§ 4. Returns to Paris. — Egyptian Expedition. — Invasion of Syria. — Return to France . . . 62
§ 5. Revolution of Brumaire 73

CHAPTER III.

THE FIRST CONSUL.

	PAGE
§ 1. Becomes First Consul	83
§ 2. His Jealousy of Moreau. — Campaign of Marengo. — Treaty of Lunéville. — The Concordat. — Treaty of Amiens	88
§ 3. Reconstruction of French Institutions. — Gradual Progress towards Monarchy. — Nivose	97
§ 4. Rupture with England. — Execution of the Duc d'Enghien. — The Emperor Napoleon. — Trial of Moreau	105

CHAPTER IV.

THE EMPEROR.

§ 1. Designs against England and the Continent. — Napoleon Crowned	116
§ 2. Campaign against Austria and Russia. — Capitulation of Ulm. — Battle of Austerlitz. — War with Prussia. — Jena and Auerstädt. — Eylau. — Friedland. — Treaty of Tilsit	123
§ 3. Napoleon as King of Kings	135

CHAPTER V.

REBELLION.

§ 1. French Army in Spain. — Popular Rising in Spain. — Napoleon in Spain	145
§ 2. First German War of Liberation. — Ratisbon. — Aspern. — Wagram. — Treaty of Schönbrunn.	

Contents. xi

— War with Russia impending. — Divorce of Josephine. — Marriage with Marie Louise . . 154
§ 3. Annexation of Holland. — Dissolution of the Alliance of Tilsit. — Invasion of Russia . . . 164
§ 4. In Poland. — Niemen crossed. — Smolensk. — Battle of Borodino. — Burning of Moscow. — Retreat from Moscow 171

CHAPTER VI.

FALL OF NAPOLEON.

§ 1. Wars of 1813-1814. — War with Russia and Prussia. — Relations to Austria 182
§ 2. War with Russia, Prussia, and Austria 195
§ 3. Invasion of France by the Allies. — Napoleon abdicates 201
§ 4. He retires to Elba. — Disquiet in France. — The Hundred Days. — Battle of Waterloo . . . 211
§ 5. The Second Abdication. — Surrender to England. — Exile in St. Helena. — Autobiography. — Death 224

NAPOLEON'S PLACE IN HISTORY.

CHAPTER I.

HOW FAR NAPOLEON WAS FAVORED BY CIRCUMSTANCES.

§ 1. His Rise to Power 240
§ 2. His Ascendency in Europe 243
§ 3. His Conquests 245
§ 4. Was he Invincible? 249

CHAPTER II.

HOW FAR NAPOLEON WAS SHAPED BY CIRCUMSTANCES.

	PAGE
§ 1. His Lawlessness	254
§ 2. His Impressibility	263
§ 3. His Relation to Parties	265
§ 4. His Significance in French History	268

CHAPTER III.

WHAT NAPOLEON WAS IN HIMSELF.

§ 1. What was his Plan?	279
§ 2. Origin of the Plan	286
§ 3. Execution of the Plan	291
§ 4. Was he successful?	295
§ 5. How far his Influence was Beneficial	299
§ 6. Napoleon judged by his Plan	303

A SHORT HISTORY

OF

NAPOLEON THE FIRST.

CHAPTER I.

BUONAPARTE.

§ 1. *Date of Buonaparte's Birth. — Military Education. — Early Authorship.*

THE family Buonaparte (so the name is written by Napoleon's father and by himself down to 1796, though the other spelling occurs in early Italian documents) was of Tuscan origin. A branch of it was settled in Corsica at least as early as the sixteenth century, from which time the Buonapartes appear as influential citizens of Ajaccio. They had an ancient title of nobility from the Genoese republic, and Napoleon's grandfather obtained letters of nobility also from the Grand Duke of Tuscany. They had therefore the right to sign De Buonaparte, but ordinarily dropped the preposition of honor. Charles Marie de Buonaparte (who was born in 1746, and studied law at the University of Pisa, where he took his doctor's degree in 1769) married at the age of eighteen Letitia Ramolino, who was not quite fifteen. The lady had beauty, but apparently neither rank nor wealth. In the children of this marriage the father, a somewhat indolent Italian gentleman with a certain taste for literature, seems traceable in Joseph, Jerome, and partly also in Lucien; the energy of which Lucien had a share, which Caroline also displayed, and which astonished the world in Napoleon, is perhaps attributable to the Corsican blood of the mother. Thirteen children were born, of whom eight grew up. The list of these is as follows: Joseph (king, first of Naples, then of Spain), *Napoleon*, Lucien, Eliza (Princess Bacciochi), Pauline (married, first to General Leclerc, afterwards to Prince Borghese), Caroline (married to Murat, became queen of Naples), Louis (king of Holland), Jerome (king of Westphalia). Of these the eldest was born in 1768, the youngest in 1784.

Besides his brothers and sisters, Napoleon raised to importance Joseph Fesch, half-brother of his mother, a Swiss on the father's side, who was afterwards known to the world as Cardinal Fesch.

It is the accepted opinion that Napoleon was born at Ajaccio on August 15, 1769. This opinion rests indeed on the positive statement of Joseph, but it is certain from documents that on January 7, 1768, Madame Letitia bore a son at Corte, who was baptized by the name of Nabulione. And even in legal documents we find contradictory statements about the time and place of birth, not only of Napoleon, but also of Joseph. It has been suggested that all difficulties disappear at once if we suppose that Napoleon and Nabulione were one and the same, and that Joseph was really the second son, whom the parents found it convenient to pass off as the first-born. This they may have found convenient when, in 1779, they gained admission for a son to the military school of Brienne. A son born in 1768 would at that date be inadmissible, as being above ten years of age. On this supposition Napoleon was introduced by a fraud to that military career which changed the face of the world! Nevertheless it is certain from Lucien's memoir that of such a fraud nothing was known to the younger members of the family, who regarded Joseph as without doubt the eldest.

After passing two or three months in a school at Autun for the purpose of learning French — he had hitherto been a thorough Italian — Napoleon entered Brienne on April 23 or 25, 1779, where he remained for more than five years, and then in October, 1784, passed, as 'cadet-gentilhomme,' into the military school of Paris. In the next year, 1785, he obtained his commission of lieutenant in the regiment La Fère, stationed at Valence. He had already lost his father, who, undertaking a journey to France on business, was entertained at Montpellier in the house of an old Corsican friend, Madame Permon, mother of the celebrated memoir-writer Madame Junot, and died there of the disease which was afterwards fatal to Napoleon, on February 24, 1785, at the age of thirty-eight years.

The fact principally to be noticed about Napoleon's extraction and boyhood is that he was by birth a noble, needy and provincial, and that from his tenth year his education was exclusively military. Of all the great rulers of the world none has been by breeding so purely a military specialist. He could scarcely remember the time when he was not a soldier living among soldiers. The effects of this training showed themselves too evidently when he had risen to the head of affairs. At the same time poverty in a society of luxurious noblemen, and the consciousness of foreign birth and of ignorance of the French language, made his school life at times very unhappy. At one time he demands passionately to be taken away, at another time he sends in a memorial, in which he argues the expediency of subjecting the cadets to a more Spartan diet. His character declared itself earlier than his talents. He was reported as 'taciturn, fond of solitude, capricious, haughty, extremely disposed to egoism, seldom speaking, energetic in his answers, ready and sharp in repartee, full of self-love, ambitious, and of unbounded aspirations.' So he appeared to his teachers, and in some stories, probably exaggerated, he is represented as a complete Timon, living as a hermit, and perpetually at war with his school-fellows. His abilities do not seem to have excited wonder, but he was studious, and in mathematics and geography made great progress. He never, however, so Carnot tells us, became a truly scientific man. He had neither taste nor talent for grammatical studies, but was fond of books, and books of a solid kind. Of the writers of the day he seems to have been chiefly influenced by Rousseau and Raynal.

He is now a lieutenant of artillery in the service of Louis XVI. The next years are spent mainly with his regiment at Valence, Lyons, Douai, Paris,

Auxonne, Seurre, Auxonne again. But he takes long holidays with his family at Ajaccio, obtaining permission on the ground of ill health. Thus he was at Ajaccio in 1787 from February to October, again from December, 1787, to May, 1788, again from September, 1789, to February, 1791. During this period he is principally engaged in authorship, being consumed by the desire of distinction, and having as yet no other means of attaining it. He produces 'Letters on the History of Corsica,' which he proposes at first to dedicate to Paoli, later to Raynal; he competes for a prize offered by the Academy of Lyons for the best essay written 'to determine the truths and feelings which it is most important to inculcate on men for their happiness.' Among his smaller compositions is 'The Narrative of the Masked Prophet.' Of all these writings, which are to be distinguished from the pamphlets written by him with a practical object, it may be said that they show more character than literary ability. As the compositions of a boy they are indeed remarkable for their precocious seriousness; but what strikes the reader most in them is a sort of suppressed passion that marks the style, a fierce impatience, as if the writer knew already how much he had to get through in a short life. But his sentiments, love of liberty, of virtue, of domestic happiness, are hollow, and his affectation of tenderness even ridiculous. The essay, as a composition, is positively bad, and was naturally unsuccessful.

§ 2. *Corsican Period.*

Meanwhile his active life had begun with the Revolution of 1789. The first chapter of it is separate from the rest, and leads to nothing. That astonishing career, which has all the unity of a most thrilling drama, does not begin till 1795. The six years which preceded it may be called his Corsican period, because for the greater part of it he may be thought to have regarded Corsica as the destined scene of his future life. It must be very summarily treated here.

In 1789 the Italian island of Corsica had been for twenty years a dependency of France. But France had acquired it in a most unscrupulous manner by purchasing the rights of the republic of Genoa over it. She did this in 1768, that is, when Corsica had contested those rights in a war of nearly forty years, and had been practically independent and happy for about thirteen years under the dictatorship of Pasquale Paoli. It was an act similar to the partition of Poland, and seems to mark a design on the part of France —

which had just suffered great colonial losses — to extend her power by way of the Mediterranean into the East. Paoli was compelled to take refuge in England, where he was still living when the French Revolution broke out. In the fall of Corsica a certain Matteo Buttafuoco played a disgraceful part. He had been sent by Paoli to treat as plenipotentiary with France, was won over by Choiseul, declared against the national cause, and appeared in the island as colonel of Louis XV.'s Corsican regiment. He too was still living when the States-General met, and represented there the *noblesse* of Corsica, while Salicetti, a name of no little prominence in the Revolution, was one of the representatives of the Corsican *tiers état*.

The Revolution was almost as dangerous an event to the relation between France and Corsica as to that between France and St. Domingo. Would the island assert its independence, and if so, could the Assembly deny its right to do this? The islanders and the exiled Paoli at their head took a moderate view. France must guarantee a good deal of local freedom; on such conditions, they thought, the relation might continue, if only to prevent the republic of Genoa from reviving its pretensions. Accordingly, on November 30, 1789, Corsica was declared by the National

Assembly to be a province of France on the motion of Salicetti himself, and the protest against this decree made by Genoa was treated with contempt. Paoli left London, was received in France with an ovation, appeared before the National Assembly on April 22, 1790, where he received the honors of the sitting, and landed in Corsica on July 14, after an absence of twenty-one years. Thus was Corsica reconciled to France by the Revolution of 1789; but the good work was undone by the Second Revolution of 1792.

Since 1769 the French power in the island had rested mainly on the *noblesse* and clergy. The Buonaparte family, as noble, had been on the unpatriotic side; Napoleon's father appears always as a courtier of the French governor Marbœuf and as a mendicant at Versailles; Madame Letitia in soliciting a place for her son Louis styles herself 'the widow of a man who always served the king in the administration of the affairs of the island of Corsica.' It is therefore a remarkable fact that, almost immediately after the taking of the Bastille, Napoleon hurried to Ajaccio and placed himself at the head of the revolutionary party with all the decision characteristic of him. He devoted himself to the establishment of a National Guard, of which he might hope to be the La

Fayette, and he published a letter to Buttafuoco, which, properly understood, is a solemn desertion of the principles of his family, similar to that of Mirabeau. This letter has all the intensity of his other early writings, but far more effectiveness. It lashes Buttafuoco for his treason of 1768, describing him as a cynic, who had no belief in virtue, but supposed all men to be guided by selfish interest. The invective has lost its edge for us who know that the author soon after openly professed this very creed. In declaring for the Revolution he obeyed the real inclination of his feelings at the time, as we may see from his writings, which are in the revolutionary tone of Raynal. But had he not really, we may ask, an ulterior object, — viz. to make Corsica independent of France, and to restore the old rule of Paoli, aiming himself at Paoli's succession? Probably he wished to see such a result, but he had always two strings to his bow. In his letter to Buttafuoco he carefully avoids separating Corsican liberty from the liberty offered by the French Revolution. Had the opportunity offered, he might no doubt have stood forth at this time as the liberator of Corsica ; but circumstances did not prove favorable, and he drifted gradually in quite the opposite direction.

In October, 1790, he met Paoli at Orezza, where Corsica constituted itself as a French department, Paoli being president, Salicetti procureur-général syndic, Arena and Pozzo di Borgo (also from Ajaccio) members of the Directorium. Paoli is said to have hailed Napoleon as 'one of Plutarch's men.' As the only Corsican officer trained at a royal military school, Napoleon might aspire to become commander of a paid native guard which it was proposed to create for the island. But France had misgivings about the use to which such a guard might be put, and the Minister of War rejected the proposal. In the next year, however, he was successful in a second attempt to get the command of an armed force in Corsica, and betrayed in the course of this attempt how much more intent he was at this time upon Corsican than upon French affairs. It was decided to create four battalions of national volunteers for Corsica, and Napoleon became candidate for the post of lieutenant-colonel in the district of Ajaccio. The choice was in the hands of the volunteers themselves, and in pursuing his canvass Napoleon did not hesitate to outstay his furlough, and thus to forfeit his French commission by wilful absence from a great review of the whole French army which was appointed for the opening day of 1792.

He was, however, elected, having, it is said, executed the first of his many *coups d'état* by violently imprisoning a commissioner sent down to superintend the election. We can understand his eagerness when we remark that anarchy in Corsica was steadily increasing, so that he may have believed that the moment for some military stroke was at hand. He did not long delay. At the Easter festival of 1792 he tried to get possession of Ajaccio under cover of a tumult between the volunteers and the refractory clergy. The stroke failed, and he fled from the island. The European war was just breaking out, and at Paris everything was in confusion; otherwise he would probably have been tried by court-martial and shot.

A rebel in Corsica, a deserter in France, what was he to do? He went to Paris, where he arrived on May 21. The Second Revolution was at hand, and he could observe while no one had leisure to observe him. He witnessed the 10th of August and the downfall of the monarchy. To him this revolution was a fortunate event, for the new Government, attacked by all Europe, could not dispense with the few trained officers whom the emigration had left. On August 30 his name was restored to the army list with the rank of captain, a commission dated back to February 6, and arrears of pay. He was saved from the most desperate condition to which he was ever in his whole life reduced. On September 2 (terrible date!) he is engaged in withdrawing his sister Eliza from St. Cyr (the House of St. Louis having been suppressed). The next step he takes is remarkable. The great war which was to carry him to the pinnacle of fame was now in full progress. By undeserved good luck his military rank is restored to him. Will he not hurry to his regiment, eager to give proof of his military talents? No, his thoughts are still in Corsica. On the pretext of conducting his sister to her home he sets off without delay for Ajaccio, where he arrives on the 17th. The winter was spent in the unsuccessful expedition, which may be called Napoleon's first campaign, made from Corsica against the island of Sardinia. On his return he found a new scene opened. The Second Revolution was beginning to produce its effect in Corsica, which was no mere province of France, and in which everything was modified by the presence of Paoli. Elsewhere the Convention was able by its Representatives in Mission to crush opposition, but they could not so crush Corsica and Paoli. There was thus a natural opposition between the Convention and Paoli, and the islanders began to fall into opposite parties, as adherents of the former or of the latter. It might have been expected that Bonaparte, who all his life had glorified Paoli, and whose early letters are full of hatred to France, would have been an enthusiastic Paolist. But a breach seems to have taken place between them soon after Napoleon's return from Paris, perhaps in consequence of his escapade of Easter, 1792. The crisis came on April 2, when Paoli was denounced before the Convention, among others by Marat, and it was decreed that he and Pozzo di Borgo should come to Paris and render an account of their conduct to the Convention. Paoli refused, but, with the remarkable, perhaps excessive, moderation which characterized him, offered to leave Corsica if his presence there appeared to the Convention undesirable. The islanders however rallied round him almost as one man.

There could be no reason why the horrors of the Second Revolution should extend to Corsica, even if we consider them to have been inevitable in France. For a Corsican patriot no fairer opportunity could offer of dissolving with universal approbation the connection with France which had begun in 1769. Napoleon took the opposite side. He stood out with Salicetti as the leading champion of the French connection and the bitterest opponent of Paoli. Was his motive envy, or the bitterness caused by a recent personal quarrel with Paoli? We cannot positively say, but we can form an estimate of the depth of that insular patriotism which fills the 'Letters on the History of Corsica.' Paoli summoned a national consulta at the end of May, and the dissolution of the French connection now began. The consulta denounced the Buonaparte family by name. Napoleon answered by desperate attempts to execute his old plan of getting possession of the citadel of Ajaccio. But he failed, and the whole family, with Madame Letitia and Fesch, pursued by the fury of the people, took refuge in France. With this Hijra the first period of Napoleon comes to an end.

§ 3. *At Toulon.—Joins the Army of Italy.—Connection with the Robespierres.—Ordered to the Army of the West.—Remains in Paris.*

Up to this time Napoleon has regarded the French nation with dislike, French ways and habits as strange and foreign, and he has more than once turned aside from a French career when it seemed open to him. Henceforth he has no other career to look for, unless indeed it may be possible, as for some time he continued to hope, to make his way back to Corsica by means of French arms. A certain change seems now to pass over his character. Up to this time his writings, along with their intensity, have had a highly moral and sentimental tone. He seems sincerely to have thought himself not only stronger and greater but better than other men. At school he found himself among school-fellows who were 'a hundred fathoms below the noble sentiments which animated himself,' and again much later he pronounced that 'the men among whom he lived had ways of thinking as different from his own as moonlight is from sunlight.' Probably he still felt that he had more vivid thoughts than other men, but he ceases henceforth to be a moralist. His next pamphlet, 'Le Souper de Beaucaire,' is entirely free from sentiment, and in a very short time he appears as a cynic, and even pushing cynicism to an extreme.

It was in June, 1793, that the whole family found themselves at Toulon in the midst of the Corsican emigration. France was in a condition not less disturbed than Corsica, for it was the moment of the fall of the Girondins. Plunged into this new party strife, Napoleon could hardly avoid taking the side of the Mountain. Paoli had been in a manner the Girondin of Corsica, and Napoleon had headed the opposition to him. In 'Le

Souper de Beaucaire' (published in August, 1793), which is the manifesto of this period, as the 'Letter to Buttafuoco' is of the earlier period, he himself compares the Girondins to Paoli, and professes to think that the safety of the state requires a deeper kind of republicanism than theirs. The immediate occasion of this pamphlet is the civil war of the South, into which he was now plunged. Marseilles had declared against the Convention, and had sent an army under Rousselet which had occupied Avignon, but had evacuated it speedily on being attacked by the troops of the Mountain under Carteaux. Napoleon took part in the attack, commanding the artillery, but it seems an unfounded statement that he specially distinguished himself. This was in July, and a month later the pamphlet was written. It is a dialogue between inhabitants of Marseilles, Nimes, and Montpellier and a military man. It is highly characteristic, full of keen and sarcastic sagacity, and of clear military views; but the temperature of its author's mind has evidently fallen suddenly; it has no warmth, but a remarkable cynical coldness. Among the Representatives in Mission recently arrived at Avignon was the younger Robespierre, with whom Salicetti was intimate. Napoleon, introduced by Salicetti and recommended by this pamphlet, naturally rose high in his favor. We must not be misled by the violence with which, as First Consul, he attacked this party, and the horror he then professed to feel for their crimes, so as to conclude that his connection with the Jacobins, and especially the Robespierres, was at the beginning purely accidental and professional. What contemporary evidence we have exhibits Buonaparte at this time as holding the language of a terrorist, and we shall see how narrowly he escaped perishing with the Robespierres in Thermidor. Of course it is not necessary to disbelieve Marmont, when he says that the atrocities of the Robespierrists were never to Napoleon's taste, and that he did much to check them within the sphere of his influence.

He marched with Carteaux into Marseilles late in August, and about the same time Toulon delivered itself into the hands of the English. Just at this moment he was promoted to the rank of *chef de bataillon* in the second regiment of artillery, which gave him practically the command of the artillery in the force which was now formed to besiege Toulon. The story of his relations with the generals who were sent successively to conduct the siege, Carteaux the painter, Doppet the physician, Dugommier the brave veteran, and of his discovery of the true way to take Toulon, are perhaps somewhat legendary, but he may probably have been eloquent and persuasive at the council of war held on November 25, in which the plan of the siege was laid down. That he distinguished himself in action is more certain, for Dugommier writes: 'Among those who distinguished themselves most, and who most aided me to rally the troops and push them forward, are Citizens Buona Parte, commanding the artillery, Arena and Cervoni, adjutants-general' (*Moniteur*, December 7, 1793). He was now named general of brigade.

He now passes out of the civil into the foreign war. The military system of the Convention is by this time in full operation. Distinct armies face each enemy, and the great military names of the Revolution are already in men's mouths. The Army of the North has Jourdan, Leclerc, Vandamme, Brune, Mortier; that of the Moselle has Hoche, Bessières, Moreau; that of the Rhine, Pichegru, Schérer, Berthier; that of the West, Marceau and Kléber. Buonaparte joins the Army of Italy as general of artillery and inspector-general; to the same army is attached Masséna as general of division; Dumerbion is general-in-chief. It is now that for the first time we find the young man's exceptional ability remarked. Restless

pushing ambition he had shown all along, but that
he was more than a mere intriguer seems to have
been first discerned by the younger Robespierre,
who in a letter of April 5, 1794, describes him as
'of transcendent merit.' In the brief campaign of
the Army of Italy which occupied the month of
July, 1794, he took no part, while Masséna commanded in the illness of Dumerbion. But in July
he made his first essay in diplomacy. Genoa was
among the earliest of the many feeble neutral
states which suffered in the conflict of the Revolution with the Great Powers, and at the expense
of which the revolutionary empire was founded.
Bonaparte was sent by the younger Robespierre to
remonstrate with the Genoese Government upon
the use which they suffered the Coalition to make
of their neutral territory. He was in Genoa from
July 16 to July 23; he urged the French claim with
success; he returned to Nice on July 28. But July
28, 1794, is the 9th Thermidor, on which his patron
perished with the elder Robespierre on the scaffold.

Probably the connection of Napoleon with the
Robespierres was closer than he himself at a later
time liked to have it thought. 'He was their man,
their plan-maker,' writes Salicetti; 'he had acquired an ascendency over the Representatives
(*i.e.* especially Robespierre junior) which it is

impossible to describe,' writes Marmont. Accordingly after Thermidor the Representatives in Mission who remained with the Army of Italy — viz. Salicetti, Albitte, and Laporte — suspended Bonaparte from his functions, and placed him provisionally under arrest (August 6). He was imprisoned at the Fort Carré near Antibes, but fortunately for him was not sent to Paris. On the 20th he was set provisionally at liberty on the ground of 'the possible utility of the military and local knowledge of the said *Bonaparte.*' This spelling begins already to creep in.

His escape was due, according to Marmont, to Salicetti's favor and to the powerful help he himself succeeded in procuring; 'he moved heaven and earth.' His power of attaching followers also now begins to appear; Junot and Marmont, who had become acquainted with him at Toulon, were prepared, if he had been sent to Paris, to set him free by killing the *gens d'armes* and carrying him into the Genoese territory. Marmont has graphically described the influence exerted upon himself at this time by Napoleon; 'there was so much future in his mind,' he writes.

This was a passing check; early in 1795 he suffered a greater misfortune. He had been engaged in a maritime expedition of which the object was to recover Corsica, now completely in the power of the English. On March 3 he embarked with his brother Louis, Marmont, and others on the brig 'Amitié.' On the 11th the fleet set sail. It fell in with the English, lost two ships, and returned defeated. The enterprise was abandoned, and by the end of the same month we find Lacombe Saint-Michel, member of the Committee of Public Safety, sending orders to the General of Brigade Bonaparte, to proceed immediately to the Army of the West in order to take command of the artillery there. He left Marseilles for Paris on May 5, feeling that all the ground gained by his activity at Toulon, and by the admiration he had begun to inspire, was lost again, that his career was all to recommence, and in peculiarly unfavorable circumstances.

This may almost be called the last ill turn he ever received from fortune. It has been attributed to the Girondist spite of a certain Aubry against the Montagnard Bonaparte. The truth seems rather to be that the Committee of Public Safety felt that the Corsican element was too strong in the Army of Italy; they remarked that 'the patriotism of these refugees is less manifest than their disposition to enrich themselves.' Lacombe Saint-Michel knew Corsica; and the new general of the Army of Italy, Schérer, remarks of Bonaparte just at this moment that 'he is a really good artillerist, but has rather too much ambition and intrigue for his advancement.'

The anecdote told by Bonaparte himself of his ordering an attack of outposts in order to treat a lady to a sight of real war, 'how the French were successful, but necessarily no result could come of it, the attack being a pure fancy, and yet some men were left on the field,' belongs to the last months of his service in the Army of Italy. It is worthy of notice, as showing his cynical insensibility, that he acted thus almost at the very beginning of his military career, and not when he had been hardened by long familiarity with bloodshed. On his arrival at Paris he avoids proceeding to the Army of the West, and after a time obtains from Doulcet de Pontécoulant a post in the topographical section of the War Office. Here he has an opportunity of resuming his old work, and we find him furnishing Doulcet, as he had before furnished Robespierre junior, with strategical plans for the conduct of the war in Italy. Late in August he applies for a commission from Government to go to Constantinople at the head of a party of artillerists in order to reform that department of the Turkish service. He sends in a testimonial from Doulcet which describes him as 'a citizen who may be usefully employed whether in the artillery or in any other arm, and even in the department of foreign affairs.' But at this moment occurs the crisis of his life. It coincides with a remarkable crisis in the history of France.

§ 4. *Checks Revolt of the Sections. — Marriage. — Commander of Army of Italy.*

The Second Revolution (1792) had destroyed the monarchy, but a republic, properly speaking, had not yet been established. Between 1792 and 1795 the government had been provisionally in the hands of the National Convention, which had been summoned, not to govern, but to create a new constitution. Now at length, the danger from foreign enemies having been averted, the Convention could proceed to its proper work of establishing a definitive republic.

But there was danger lest the country, when appealed to, should elect to undo the work of 1792 by recalling the Bourbons, or at least should avenge on the Mountain the atrocities of the Terror. To preserve the continuity of government an expedient was adopted. As under the new constitution the assemblies were to be renewed periodically to the extent only of one-third at a time, it was decreed that the existing Convention should be treated as the first Corps Législatif under the new system. Thus, instead of being dissolved and making way for new assemblies, it was to form the nucleus of the new legislature, and to be renewed only to the extent of one-third. This additional law, which was promulgated along with the new constitution, excited a rebellion in Paris. The sections (or wards) called into existence a revolutionary assembly, which met at the Odéon. This the Convention suppressed by military force, and the discontent of the individual sections was thereby increased. At the same time their confidence was heightened by a check they inflicted upon General Menou, who, in attempting to disarm the section Lepelletier, was imprisoned in the Rue Vivienne, and could only extricate himself by concluding a sort of capitulation with the insurgents. Thereupon the Convention, alarmed, put Menou under arrest, and gave the command of the armed force of Paris and of the Army of the Interior to Barras, a leading politician of the day, who had acquired a sort of military reputation by having held several times the post of Representative in Mission. Barras knew the Army of Italy and the services which Buonaparte had rendered at Toulon, and nominated him second in command.

It does not seem that Buonaparte showed any remarkable firmness of character or originality of genius in meeting the revolt of the sections on the next day (Vendémiaire 13 — *i.e.* October 5) with grape-shot. The disgrace of Menou was a warning that the Convention required decisive action, and the invidiousness of the act fell upon Barras, not upon Bonaparte. Indeed in the official report drawn by Bonaparte himself his own name scarcely appears; instead of assuming courageously the responsibility of the deed, he took great pains to shirk it. He appeared in the matter merely as the instrument, as the skilful artillerist, by whom Barras and the Convention carried their resolute policy into effect. Moreover, though his arrangements were able, there seems no truth in the story of his despatching Murat at two o'clock in the morning to bring up artillery from Sablons. It will be observed that on this occasion he defends the cause of Jacobinism. This does not require to be explained, as at a later time he took much pains to explain it, by the consideration that, odious as Jacobinism was, on the particular occasion it was identified with 'the great truths of our Revolution.' The truth is that in his first years he appears uniformly as a Jacobin. He was at the moment an official in the Jacobin Government, and speaks in his letters of the party of the sections just as a Government official might be expected to do.

In this affair he produced an impression of real military capacity among the leading men of France, and placed Barras himself under a personal obligation. He was rewarded by being appointed in succession to Barras, who now resigned, commander of the Army of the Interior. In this position, political and military at the same time, he preluded to the part reserved for him later of First Consul and Emperor. He also strengthened his new position materially by his marriage with Josephine de Beauharnais *née* Tascher. His first choice had been the friend of his family, Mme. Permon, who, however, rejected him. The legend tells of a youth calling upon him to claim the sword of his father, guillotined in the Terror, of Napoleon treating the youth kindly, of his mother paying a visit of thanks, of an attachment following. But even if he was really attached to Josephine, we must not think of the match as one of mere unworldly affection. It was scarcely less splendid for the young General Bonaparte than his second match was for the Emperor Napoleon. Josephine was prominent in Parisian society, and for the lonely Corsican, so completely without connections in

Paris or even in France, such an alliance was of priceless value. She had not much either of character or intellect, but real sweetness of disposition. Her personal charm was not so much that of beauty as of grace, social tact, and taste in dress. The act of marriage is dated Ventose 19, Year IV. (*i.e.* March 9, 1796), and is remarkable because it declares Napoleon to have been born in 1768 instead of 1769, and Josephine in 1767 instead of 1763. On this day he had already been appointed to the command of the Army of Italy. His great European career now begins.

CHAPTER II.

GENERAL BONAPARTE.

——— § 1. *Italian Campaign.*

THE fifth year of the Revolutionary War was opening. It was already evident that this war would change the face of Europe, and almost certain that it would create a new French ascendency. The Coalition, which in 1793 seemed to have France at its mercy, had been paralyzed by the reopening of the Polish question in its rear. Prussian troops were recalled from the Rhine to oppose Kosciuszko, and, at the same time, the mutual jealousy of Prussia and Austria, which had dominated German politics for half a century, was suddenly rekindled. France reaped the benefit of this diversion. In the campaign of 1794 she expelled the Austrians from Belgium, in the following winter she overran Holland, expelled the Stadtholder, established the authority of the so-called Patriots, and thus wrested this state from the Coalition. No similar blows had been struck by France since the age of Louis XIV., and, what was still more portentous, the Coalition, instead of rallying its forces, began at this moment rapidly to dissolve. Thus the system of Europe was already broken up. A new age had begun in which France stood forth as a conquering Power, her territory already enlarged, her military spirit exalted, her army increased and disciplined, beyond all former experience. Bonaparte did not introduce, but found already introduced, the principle of conquest.

Prussia, with most of the North German princes, had retired from the war in April, 1795; Spain followed the example in July. The Coalition assumes its second shape, which it was to keep almost till the pacification of 1801; it is now a Triple Alliance of Russia, Austria and England; and Russia as yet is an inactive, not to say a perfidious, member of it. Practically France has to deal on the Continent only with Austria, who in the campaign of 1795 shielded Germany against the invasion of Jourdan and Pichegru. The French are already conquerors, but in this campaign they meet with ill-fortune. At the moment when Vendémiaire revealed Bonaparte to the world, Clerfait and Wurmser were striking blows which forced the French armies to recross the Rhine and for the moment saved Germany. But only Bonaparte has quite firmly grasped the truth that there is no real enemy but Austria, for, though all can see that Prussia has deserted her on the Rhine, it seems that Sardinia still stands by her in the Alps. Bonaparte is sure that Sardinia will sustain Austria as little as Prussia had done, and has as little interest to continue the war, now that she has lost Savoy and Nice, and sees France stronger than ever. Can Sardinia but be pushed aside, Austria may be attacked in Lombardy, where she is an alien power. Bonaparte has long pictured himself rousing the Italian population against her, driving her across the Alps, and co-operating with the Army of the Rhine by an attack in flank. Since Vendémiaire he had discussed this plan with Carnot, who was now one of the five Directors, and it was perhaps Carnot — at least so we are told in the *Réponse à Bailleul* — who procured Bonaparte's appointment to the Italian command.

At the moment the French armies everywhere were paralyzed by financial need; it seemed likely that in 1796 France would achieve nothing for want of means. For this difficulty also Bonaparte had a resource. From the outset the French had levied contributions in the territories they invaded. By frankly adopting this system, by making war support war, Bonaparte would turn poverty itself into a spur and a warlike motive. He announced to the army without the least disguise: 'Soldiers, —You are naked and ill fed; I will lead you into the most fruitful plains in the world. Rich provinces, great cities will be in your power. There you will find honor, and fame, and wealth.' The French soldier thus received at the same time a touch of the wolf, which made him irresistible, and a touch of the mercenary, which made him in the end useful to Bonaparte.

This order of the day was issued from Nice on March 27. The campaign began early in April. This, the first of Bonaparte's campaigns, has been compared to his last. As in 1815 he tried to separate Blücher and Wellington, hoping to overcome them in turn, so now with more success he attacked first the Austrians under Beaulieu and then the Sardinians under Colli. Defeating the Austrians at Montenotte, Millesimo, and Dego, he turned on the 15th against Colli, defeated him at Ceva and again at Mondovi. Almost in a moment the calculation of Bonaparte was justified. Sardinia, which might have made a long and obstinate defence behind the fortifications of Turin, Alexandria and Tortona, retired at once from an alliance of which she was weary. She signed the convention of Cherasco on the 28th, yielding her principal fortresses into the hands of France. What Bonaparte had so long dreamed of he accomplished in a single month, and turned himself at once to the conquest of Lombardy.

The month of May was devoted to the invasion. On the 7th he crossed the Po at Piacenza, stormed the bridge over the Adda at Lodi on the 10th, and, as the Archduke who governed Lombardy had quitted Milan on the 9th, retiring by Bergamo into Germany, Bonaparte entered Milan on the 15th. That day Bonaparte told Marmont that his success hitherto was nothing to what was reserved for him. 'In our days,' he added, 'no one has conceived anything great; it falls to me to give the example.' June was spent in consolidating the conquest of Lombardy, in spoiling the country, and repressing the insurrections which broke out among the Italians, astonished to find themselves plundered by their 'liberators.' From the middle of July the war, as far as Austria is concerned, becomes a war for Mantua. Austria makes desperate and repeated efforts to raise the siege of this all-important fortress. In June she withdraws from the Rhine one of her armies and a general who had won renown in the preceding campaign, Wurmser. He arrives at Innspruck on June 26th; here in Tyrol he assembles 50,000 men.

At the end of July he advances on both sides of the Lake of Garda, and threatens Bonaparte's communications by occupying Brescia. Bonaparte abandoned the siege of Mantua, and brought his whole force to meet the enemy. The position for a moment seemed desperate. He called councils of war, and declared in favor of retreating across the Adda. When Augereau resisted this determination, he left the room declaring that he would have nothing to do with the matter, and, when Augereau asked who was to give orders, answered 'You!' The desperate course was rewarded with success. The Austrians were defeated at Castiglione on August 3, and retired into Tyrol. But Mantua had been revictualled, and Bonaparte had suffered the loss of his siege-train.

Early in September Bonaparte, having received reinforcements from France, assumed the offensive against Wurmser, and after defeating him at Bassano forced him to throw himself with the remainder of his army into Mantua (September 15).

At the end of October Austria had assembled a new army of 50,000 men, mostly, however, raw recruits. They were placed under the command of Allvintzy. Bonaparte was to be overwhelmed between this army and that of Wurmser issuing from Mantua. But by a night march he fell upon

Allvintzy's rear at Arcole. The surprise failed, and Bonaparte's life was at one moment in great danger. But after three days of obstinate conflict the Austrians retreated (November 15–17). From Arcole he used ever afterwards to date his profound confidence in his own fortune. Mantua, however, still held out, and early in January (1797) a fourth and last attempt was made by Allvintzy to relieve it, but he was again completely defeated at Rivoli (Jan. 14), and a whole Austrian *corps d'armée* under Provera laid down its arms at Roverbella (Jan. 16). On receiving the intelligence of this disaster Wurmser concluded the capitulation by which the French were put in possession of Mantua (Feb. 2).

§ 2. *Acts as Independent Conqueror. — Levying of Contributions. — His Italian Policy. — Advance on Austria. — Preliminaries of Leoben. — Occupation of Venice. — Coup d'État of Fructidor. — Treaty of Campo Formio.*

Such was the campaign of Bonaparte against Austria, by which he raised his reputation at once above that of all the other generals of the republic, Jourdan, Moreau, or Hoche. But he had acted by no means merely as a general of the republic against Austria. He had assumed from the beginning the part of an independent conqueror, neither bound by the orders of his Government nor by any rules of international law or morality.

The commander of a victorious army wields a force which only a Government long and firmly established can hold in check. A new Government, such as the Directory in France, having no root in the country, is powerless before a young victor such as Bonaparte. In vain the Directory devised a plan by which the Army of Italy should be divided between Bonaparte and Kellermann, while the whole diplomacy of the campaign should be intrusted to Salicetti as Commissioner. Bonaparte defeated these manœuvres as easily as those of Beaulieu and Colli. In truth the *coup d'état* of Brumaire was in his mind before he had been many weeks at the head of an army. But long before he ventured to strike the existing Government, we see that he has completely emancipated himself from it, and that his acts are those of an independent ruler, as had been those of Cæsar in Gaul or of Pompey in the East, while the Roman republic was still nominally standing. As early as June, 1796, he said to Miot, 'The commissioners of the Directory have no concern with my policy; I do what I please.'

From the outset it had been contemplated to make the invasion of Italy financially profitable. Contributions were levied so rapaciously that in the duchy of Milan, where the French had professed to appear as brothers and liberators, a rebellion against them speedily broke out, which Bonaparte suppressed with the merciless cruelty he always showed in such cases. He kept the promise of his first proclamation; he made the army rich. 'From this moment,' writes Marmont, 'the chief part of the pay and salaries was paid in coin. This led to a great change in the situation of the officers, and to a certain extent in their manners. The Army of Italy was at that time the only one which had escaped from the unprecedented misery which all the armies had so long endured.' The amount of confiscation seems to have been enormous. Besides direct contributions levied in the conquered territory, the domains of dispossessed Governments, the revenues and property of churches and hospitals, were at Bonaparte's disposal. There seems reason to think that but a small proportion of this plunder was ever accounted for. It went to the army chest, over which Bonaparte retained the control, and the pains that he took to corrupt his officers is attested in the narrative of Marmont, who relates that Bonaparte once caused a large sum to pass through his hands, and when he took great pains to render a full account of it, as the officers had then *une fleur de délicatesse*, Bonaparte blamed him for not having kept it for himself.

As he made himself financially independent of the Government, so he began to develop an independent policy. Hitherto he has had no politics, but has been content to talk the Jacobinism of the ruling party; now he takes a line, and it is not quite that of the Government. He had already, in June, 1796, invaded the Papal territory, and concluded a convention at Bologna by which he extorted fifteen millions from the Pope; immediately after the fall of Mantua he entered the States of the Church again, and concluded the treaty of Tolentino on February 19. We see how freely he combines diplomacy with war; he writes without disguise to the Directory, October 5: 'You incur the greatest risk whenever your general in Italy is not the centre of everything.' But now in dealing with the Pope he separates his policy from that of the Directory. He demands indeed the cession of Bologna, Ferrara, and the Romagna, besides Avignon and the Venaissin, and the temporary cession of Ancona. But he recognizes the Pope by treating with him, and towards the Catholic religion and the priesthood he shows himself unexpectedly merciful. Religion is not to be altered in the ceded Legations, and Bonaparte extends his protection in the most ostentatious manner to the *prêtres insermentés*, whom he found in large numbers in the States of the Church. This was the more marked as they were at this time objects of the bitterest persecution in France. Here is the first indication of the policy of the Concordat, but it is also a mark of Bonaparte's independent position, the position rather of a prince than of a responsible official; nay, it marks a deliberate intention to set himself up as a rival of the Government.

His manner of conducting the war was as unprecedented as his relation to the Government, and in like manner foreshadowed the Napoleonic period. It was not that of a civilized belligerent, but of a universal conqueror. The Revolution had put all international law into abeyance. By proclaiming a sort of crusade against monarchy it had furnished itself with a pretext for attacking almost all States alike, for almost all were either monarchical or at least aristocratic. Bonaparte in Italy, as in his later wars, knows nothing of neutrality. Thus Tuscany, the first of all states to conclude a treaty with the French republic, is not thereby saved from invasion. Bonaparte's troops march in, seize Leghorn, and take possession of all the English property found in that port. More remarkable still is the treatment of Venice. The territory of the republic is turned unceremoniously into a field of battle between France and Austria, and at the end of the war the Venetian republic is blotted out of the map.

Further is to be remarked the curious development which was given to the principle of plunder. The financial distress of France and the impoverishment of the army at the opening of the campaign might account for much simple spoliation. But the practice was now introduced of transferring pictures and statues from the Italian palaces and galleries to France. This singular revival of primitive barbaric modes of making war becomes more striking when we reflect that the spoiler of Italy was himself an Italian.

Altogether these campaigns brought to light a personality entirely without precedent in modern European history. True, the Revolution behind him and the circumstances around him were absolutely unprecedented. Marmont remarked at the time the rapid and continual development which just then showed itself in Bonaparte's character. 'Every day,' he writes, 'he seemed to see before him a new horizon.' An ambitious man had suddenly become aware that a career entirely unparalleled was open to him, if only he could find audacity and unscrupulous energy to enter upon it. Add to this that he had lived for three years in the midst of disorders and horrors such as might well have dissipated all principles, beliefs, and restraints. Even as early as the 13th Vendémiaire we find him impressed with a fatalist belief in his own luck ('I received no hurt; I am always lucky,' he writes), and there are indications that his wonderful escape at Arcole greatly heightened this belief in a mind naturally somewhat superstitious.

At this moment, as Bonaparte's private political views begin to appear, his Jacobinism, even his republicanism, slips from him like a robe. As early as May, 1797, he said to Miot and Melzi, 'Do you suppose that I triumph in Italy for the glory of the lawyers of the Directory, a Carnot or a Barras? Do you suppose I mean to found a republic? What an idea! a republic of thirty millions of people! with our morals, our vices! how is such a thing possible? The nation wants a chief, a chief covered with glory, not theories of government, phrases, ideological essays, that the French do not understand. They want some playthings; that will be enough; they will play with them and let themselves be led, always supposing they are cleverly prevented from seeing the goal towards which they are moving.' His contempt for the French, such as they had become under the influence of Versailles and the *salons* of Paris, and his opinion of their unfitness for republican institutions, was sincere; it was the opinion of a Corsican accustomed to more primitive, more masculine ways of life; we meet with it in his earliest letters, written before the thought of becoming himself the ruler of France had occurred to him.

When the fall of Mantua had established the French power in North Italy, Bonaparte's next thought was to strike at the heart of Austria from this new basis. Early in March, having secured his position in Italy by the treaty of Tolentino with Rome and by a treaty with Sardinia, he set his troops in motion. He sent Joubert with 18,000 men into Tyrol, while he prepared to march in person upon Vienna from Friuli through Carinthia and Styria. But Austria had still one resource. The year 1796, which had given Bonaparte to the French republic, had given her too a great general. The Archduke Charles, who had succeeded Clerfait in Germany, and who had been left by the departure of Wurmser for Italy utterly unable to resist the French when they advanced in June under Jourdan and Moreau, achieved in the autumn a masterpiece of strategy. About the same time that Bonaparte won the battle of Bassano, he won that of Würzburg, and by the end of October he had forced both French armies to recross the Rhine. He is now despatched to meet the other invasion, threatening Austria from the south.

But instead of being allowed to take up a strong position in the Tyrol and to await reinforcements, he was instructed to advance to Friuli, though with insufficient and demoralized troops. Bonaparte dislodged him from the line of the Tagliamento, then from that of the Isonzo, and advanced steadily until he reached Leoben in Styria on April 13. But he too felt his position to be hazardous, especially as he was not seconded by any forward movement of the Rhine armies. Hence he had himself, as early as March 31, proposed negotiation to the Archduke. At Leoben an armistice of six days was concluded.

The preliminaries of Leoben were now signed (April 18). This was the first step in a long and slippery negotiation, which led only to a renewal of the war at the end of 1798. The preliminaries afterwards suffered much modification in the treaty

of Campo Formio, which was itself soon swept
away. The prize of the war was Belgium, and
this was now ceded by Austria. In return we
might expect to find the Italian conquests of
Bonaparte restored. Instead of this a Cisalpine
republic is established, nominally independent, but
really, like the Batavian republic, under French
tutelage. Nevertheless Bonaparte, as he said himself, was in no position to dictate a peace. Accordingly he grants to Austria, as an indemnity, the
Continental possessions of the Venetian republic
as far as the Oglio, with Istria and Dalmatia.
Here is a new partition of Poland! The Venetian
republic was a neutral state, but its neutrality had
been utterly disregarded by Bonaparte during the
war, and as its territory had been freely trampled
on by his troops, irritation had necessarily arisen
among the Venetians, thence quarrels with the
French, thence on the side of the French an attack
on the aristocratic government and the setting up
of a democracy. Of all this the result was now
found to be that the Venetian empire was a conquered territory, which in her next treaty France
could cede in exchange for any desired advantage.

So far the preliminaries did not affect the Germanic empire, but only the hereditary possessions
of Austria. But they dealt also with the empire,

and here they were recklessly and, as it proved, fatally ambiguous. On the one side France conceded the integrity of the empire, on the other side the Emperor agreed to recognize the limits of France as decreed by the laws of the republic. Perhaps neither party quite knew, but perhaps both parties suspected, that these concessions were inconsistent with each other.

After so many defeats this arrangement, lawless as it was, must have seemed to Austria unexpectedly satisfactory. She had been studying for thirty years how to exchange Belgium for a province more conveniently situated. Bavaria had been her first object, but the Emperor Joseph had also cast his eyes on Venice. She had now lost Belgium by the fortune of war, but at the last moment the very equivalent she coveted was cast into her lap.

The summer of 1797 was passed by Bonaparte at Montebello, near Milan. Here he rehearsed in Italy the part of emperor, formed his court, and accustomed himself to all the functions of government. He was chiefly engaged at this time in accomplishing the dissolution of the Venetian republic. He had begun early in the spring by provoking insurrections in Brescia and Bergamo. In April the insolence of a French officer provoked a rising against the French at Salò, for which Junot, sent by Bonaparte, demanded satisfaction of the senate on the 15th. The French now attempted to disarm all the Venetian garrisons that remained on the *terra firma*, and this led to a rising at Verona, in which some hundreds of Frenchmen were massacred (April 17). On the 19th a French sea-captain, violating the customs of the port at the Lido, was fired upon from a Venetian fort. Bonaparte now declared that he would be a new Attila to Venice, and issued a manifesto in the true revolutionary style. The feeble Government could only submit. A revolution took place at Venice, and French troops took possession of the town. On May 16 a treaty was concluded by Bonaparte 'establishing peace and friendship between the French republic and the republic of Venice,' and providing that 'the French occupation should cease as soon as the new Government should declare that it no longer needed foreign assistance.' 'A principal object of this treaty,' as Bonaparte candidly explained to the Directory, 'was to obtain possession without hindrance of the city, the arsenal, and everything.' At the time that he was thus establishing friendship, he was, as we know, ceding the territory of Venice to Austria.

When we read the letters written by him at this period, we see that already, only a year after he assumed for the first time the command of an army, he has fully conceived the utmost of what he afterwards realized. Had he been shown in vision at this time what he was to be at his zenith in 1812, when he was the astonishment and terror of the world, he would probably have said that it fell short of his expectations.

In the preliminaries of Leoben such essential matters had been left unsettled or dependent on doubtful contingencies, that they were tacitly abandoned by both parties. The fall of Venice in May suggested a different arrangement. Austria might now have the town as well as the *terra firma*, and in return for this might make new concessions. As she ceased now to look to England, which was entering on a separate negotiation, she consented to accept a new basis. The second negotiation began at the end of August, and produced the Treaty of Campo Formio in the middle of October.

In return for Venice, Bonaparte is resolved to have the Rhine frontier towards Germany, and that of the Adige instead of the Oglio in Italy. But at an early stage of the conferences occurred the Revolution of Fructidor, which had the effect of reviving in the French Government the war-frenzy of the time of the Convention. The negotiation with England was broken off, and imperious orders were sent to Bonaparte to exact the utmost from Austria without ceding Venice. Much of the month of September is occupied with a struggle between the General and his Government. This ends, as might be expected, in the submission of the Directory, who are brought to see how much they need Bonaparte and how little he needs them.

On September 27 begins a new diplomatic duel, that between Bonaparte and the eminent Austrian diplomatist, Cobenzl. Bonaparte is now residing at Passariano, in a villa belonging to Doge Manin, and the conferences take place at Udine, in the neighborhood. Cobenzl contends for the integrity of the Empire, but his government is secretly prepared to barter this for a sufficient indemnity to the Austrian House in Italy. His instructions rather than Bonaparte's imperious manner caused him to yield at last, and yet the famous story of the breaking of the porcelain vase is perhaps not entirely groundless. At least the despatches of Cobenzl abound in complaints of his outrageous behavior and gasconades. At one time he 'kept on drinking glass after glass of brandy,' at another he was 'evidently drunk,' at another he confided to Cobenzl that 'he felt himself the equal of any king in the world.'

In the end he overcame both his own Government and that of Austria, and the treaty which was signed on October 17, and takes its name from the little village of Campo Formio (more correctly Campo Formido) close to Udine, practically sealed the doom of the Holy Roman Empire. It gave Venice, Istria, Dalmatia, and all Venetian territory beyond the Adige to Austria, founded the Cisalpine republic, and reserved for France, besides Belgium, Corfu and the Ionian Islands. A congress was to open at Rastatt, and Austria bound herself by a secret article to do her best to procure for France from the Germanic body the left bank of the Rhine. By retaining the Ionian Islands Bonaparte gave the first intimation of his design of opening the Eastern question.

§ 3. *The Revolution of Fructidor.*

Meanwhile a new French Revolution had taken place. A new reign of Jacobinical fanaticism had begun, which was to last till Bonaparte, who had done much to introduce it, should bring it to an end. This had happened in the following manner.

The difficulty which Bonaparte had dissipated

by his cannon in Vendémiaire had quickly returned, as it could not fail to do. A Jacobinical regicide republic had to support itself in the midst of a nation which was by no means Jacobinical, and which had representative assemblies. These assemblies, renewed by a third for the second time in the spring of 1797, placed Pichegru, suspected of royalism, in the chair of the Five Hundred, and Europe began to ask whether the restoration of the Bourbons was about to follow. Bonaparte at Montebello thought he perceived that the Austrian negotiators were bent upon delay.

The rising party was not perhaps mainly royalist; its most conspicuous representative, Carnot, the Director, was himself a regicide. In the main it aimed only at respectable government and peace, but a minority were open to some suspicion of royalism. This suspicion was fatal to the whole party, since royalism had at this time been thoroughly discredited by the follies of the *émigrés*. An outcry is raised by the soldiers. We can measure the steady progress which had been made by the military power since Vendémiaire; it had then been a tool in the hands of the Government, now it gives the law and makes the Government its tool. The armies of the Rhine, represented by Hoche, oppose the new movement; as to Bonaparte, he was driven into the same course by self-defence. Dumolard, a deputy, had called attention to his monstrous treatment of the Venetian republic, and had anticipated the judgment of history by comparing it to the partition of Poland. Bonaparte had already divulged to a friend the secret that he despised republicanism, but this attack made him once more, at least in profession, a republican and a Jacobin. It is, however, probable that he would in any case have sided with the majority of the Directory, since anything which favored the Bourbons was a hindrance to his ambition. And thus the armies of the republic stood united against the tendency of public opinion at home. Imperialism stood opposed to parliamentary government, believing itself — such was the bewilderment of the time — to be more in favor of the sovereignty of the people than the people itself, and not aware that it was paving the way for a military despot.

The catastrophe came on 18th Fructidor (September 4, 1797), when Augereau, one of Bonaparte's generals of division, who had been sent by Bonaparte to Paris, surrounded the Corps Législatif with 12,000 men and arrested the most obnoxious representatives, while another force marched to the Luxembourg, arrested the Director Barthélemi, and would have arrested Carnot had he not received warning in time to make his escape. This stroke was followed by an outrageous proscription of the new party, of whom a large number, consisting partly of members of the Councils, partly of journalists, were transported to die at Cayenne, and the elections were annulled in forty-eight departments.

Such was Fructidor, which may be considered as the third of the revolutions which compose the complex event usually known as the French Revolution. In 1789 the absolute monarchy had given place to a constitutional monarchy, which was definitively established in 1791. In 1792 the constitutional monarchy fell, giving place to a republic which was definitively established in 1795. Since 1795 it had been held that revolution was over, and that France was living under a constitution. But in Fructidor this constitution also fell, and government became revolutionary once more. It was evident that a third constitution must be established; it was evident also that this constitution must set up a military form of government — that is, an imperialism; but two more years passed before this was done.

The benefit of the change was reaped in the end by Bonaparte. Naturally he favored it and took a great share in contriving it. But it seems an exaggeration to represent him as the exclusive or even the principal author of Fructidor. Hoche took the same side as Bonaparte; Augereau outran him (and yet Augereau at this time was by no means a mere echo of Bonaparte); the division of the Army of Italy commanded by Bernadotte, which had been recently detached from the Army of Sambre-et-Meuse, and stood somewhat aloof from Bonaparte's influence, sided with him in this instance. The truth is that the rising party of Moderates gave offence to the whole military world by making peace their watchword. Outside the armies too there was profound alarm in the whole republican party, so that the circle of Madame de Staël was strongly Fructidorian, and this certainly was not guided by the influence of Bonaparte, though Madame de Staël was then among his warmest admirers. When the blow had been struck, Bonaparte knew how to reap the utmost advantage from it, and to exhibit it in its true light as mortal at the same time to the Moderates and to the republican Government itself, which now ceased to be legal and became once more revolutionary, and as favorable only to the military power and to the rising imperialism. He congratulated the armies on the fall of 'the enemies of the soldier and especially of the Army of Italy,' but accorded only the faintest approval to the Directory.

The death of Hoche, occurring soon after, removed from Bonaparte's path his only rival in the affections of the already omnipotent soldiery. Hoche alone among the generals beside Bonaparte had shown political talents; had he lived longer, he might have played with success the part in which Moreau afterwards failed.

§ 4. *Returns to Paris. — Egyptian Expedition. — Invasion of Syria. — Return to France.*

Bonaparte now left Italy, setting out from Milan on November 17, made a flying visit to Rastatt, where the congress had already assembled, and reached Paris on December 5. What next would be attempted by the man who at twenty-seven had conquered Italy and brought — momentarily at least — to an end the most memorable Continental war of modern times? From a speech delivered by him on the occasion of his reception by the Directory (Dec. 10) it appears that he had two thoughts in his mind — to make a revolution in France (' when the happiness of the French people shall be based on the best [or on better] organic laws, all Europe will become free ') and to emancipate Greece (' the two most beautiful parts of Europe, once so illustrious for arts, sciences, and the great men of whom they were the cradle, see with the loftiest hopes the genius of liberty issue from the tombs of their ancestors'). He had now some months in which to arrange the execution of these plans. The Directory, seeing no safety but in giving him employment, now committed the war with England to his charge. He becomes 'général-en-chef de l'armée d'Angleterre.' His study of internal politics soon landed him in perplexity. Should he become a Director, procuring an exemption from the rule which required the Directors to be more than forty years of age? He could decide on nothing, but felt himself unprepared to mingle in French party strife. He decided therefore that 'the pear was not ripe,' and turned again to the military schemes, which might raise his renown still higher during the year or two which the Directory would require to ruin itself. It seemed possible to combine war against England with the Oriental plan, which had been suggested to him, it is said, by Monge at Passariano. During the last war between Russia and Turkey some publicists (including Volney, an acquaintance of Bonaparte's) had recommended France to abandon her ancient alliance with the Turk and seek rather to share with Russia in his spoils. Thus was suggested to Bonaparte the thought of seizing Greece, and the dissolution of the Venetian Empire seemed to bring it within the range of practical politics. Now, as head of the Army of England, he fixed his eyes on Egypt also. In India the game was not yet quite lost for France, but England had now seized the Cape of Good Hope. To save therefore what remained of her establishments in India, France must occupy Egypt. She must not only conquer but colonize it ('if forty or fifty thousand European families fixed their industries, their laws, and their administration in Egypt, India would be presently lost to the English much more even by the force of events than by that of arms'). Such was the scheme, according to which Turkey was to be partitioned in the course of a war with England, as Venice had disappeared in the course of a war with Austria.

To this scheme it might be objected that it could scarcely fail to kindle a new European war more universal than that which had just been brought to a close. But it was already evident that the treaty of Campo Formio would lead to no real pacification. For the tide of militarism in France could not be arrested for a moment; scarcely a month passed but was marked by some

new aggression and annexation. In the spring of
1798 the old constitution of Switzerland was overthrown, French troops entered Bern and seized a
treasure of 40,000,000 francs. At the same time
a quarrel was picked with the Papal Government,
it was overthrown, the treasury plundered, and
the aged Pope, Pius VI., carried into captivity.
Thus, as Berthier said, money was furnished for
the Egyptian campaign; but on the other hand
Europe was thoroughly roused; England could
meet the threatened attack by forming a new
Coalition, and at the beginning of May, three
weeks before Bonaparte set sail, the probability
of a new Continental war was already so great
that he writes, for the benefit of General Brune, a
plan for defending Italy against an attack by a
superior force of Austrians.

But if so, was it not madness in the Directory
to banish Bonaparte along with 30,000 men and
Generals Murat, Berthier, Desaix, Kléber, Lannes,
and Marmont on the eve of a new struggle with
Europe? To us this criticism is irresistibly suggested by the event. We can see that the English
fleet barred the return of the expedition, and that
Bonaparte himself only made his way back by miraculous good fortune. But had the French Government been able to foresee this, they would have

perceived that the undertaking was not merely rash at that particular moment, but essentially impracticable. For the English fleet did not merely detain the expedition, but frustrated all its proceedings, reconquered Egypt and Malta, and forced Bonaparte to retire from Syria. It appears that the energetic interference of England was not at all anticipated. From Bonaparte's letters written on board 'L'Orient' it would seem that he scarcely realized the terrible risk he ran; it is to be considered that the superiority of the English marine had not yet been clearly proved, and that the name of Nelson was not yet redoubtable. But also it appears likely that the whole enterprise was based upon the assumption that England had retired from the Mediterranean. She had given up Corsica, and had been compelled by the alliance of the three maritime Powers, France, Spain, and Holland, to employ her whole naval force in blockading the western harbors from Cadiz to the Texel. Meanwhile France had advanced as England had retired. She controlled Corfu, Ancona, Genoa, Corsica. So much she had acquired without opposition from England, and she proceeded now with confidence to complete her empire over the Mediterranean by establishing stations at Malta and Alexandria. Bonaparte certainly did not mean to go into banishment; the vast plans which he paraded were not to be executed by himself in person, but only by the Egyptian colony which he was to found, for not only did he promise to return in October, but he actually directed his brother Joseph to prepare for him a country-house in Burgundy against the autumn. He set sail on May 19, having stimulated the zeal of his army, which he called 'one of the wings of the Army of England,' by promising that each soldier should return rich enough to buy six 'arpents' of land (the Directory were obliged to deny the genuineness of the proclamation), and, eluding Nelson, who had been driven by a storm to the island of St. Pietro near Sardinia, arrived on June 9 before Malta, where a squadron from Civita Vecchia and another from Ajaccio had preceded him. This island was in the possession of the Knights of St. John of Jerusalem, who acknowledged the King of Naples as their feudal superior and the Czar as their protector. To attack them was the direct way to involve France in war both with Naples and Russia. Bonaparte, demanding admission into the harbor for his fleet, and receiving answer that the treaties which guaranteed the neutrality of Malta permitted only the admission of four ships, attacked at once, as indeed he had been expressly commanded by the Directory to do. The people rose against the knights; the grand master, Hompesch, opened negotiations, and on the 12th Bonaparte entered La Valette. He is enthusiastic about the strength and importance of the position thus won. 'It is the strongest place in Europe; those who would dislodge us must pay dear.' He spent some days in organizing a new Government for the island, and set sail again on the 19th. On July 2 he issues his first order in Alexandria.

During the passage we find him prosecuting his earlier scheme of the emancipation of Greece. Thus from Malta he sends Lavalette with a letter to Ali Pasha of Janina. His plan therefore seems to embrace Greece and Egypt at once, and thus to take for granted the command of the sea, almost as if no English fleet existed. The miscalculation was soon made manifest. Bonaparte himself, after occupying Alexandria, set out again on the 8th and marched on Cairo; he defeated the Mamelukes first at Chebreiss and then at Embabeh, within sight of the Pyramids, where the enemy lost 2,000 and the French about 20 or 30 killed and 120 wounded. He is in Cairo on the 24th, where for the most part he remains till February of 1799. But a week after his arrival in Cairo the fleet which had brought him from France, with its admiral, Brueys, was destroyed by Nelson in Aboukir Bay. For the first time, in reporting this event to the Directory, it seems to flash on Bonaparte's mind that the English are masters of the sea. The grand design is ruined by this single stroke. France is left at war with almost all Europe, and with Turkey also (for Bonaparte's hope of deceiving the Sultan by representing himself as asserting his cause against the Mamelukes was frustrated), and her best generals with a fine army are imprisoned in another continent.

It might still be possible to produce an impression on Turkey in Asia, if not on Turkey in Europe. The Turks were preparing an army in Syria, and in February, 1799, Bonaparte anticipated their attack by invading Syria with about 12,000 men. He took El Arish on the 20th, then Gaza, and arrived before Jaffa on March 3. It was taken by assault, and a massacre commenced which, unfortunately for Bonaparte's reputation, was stopped by some officers. The consequence was that upwards of 2,000 prisoners were taken. Bonaparte, unwilling either to spare food for them or to let them go, ordered the adjutant-general to take them to the sea-shore and there shoot them, taking precautions to prevent any from escaping. This was done. 'Now,' writes Bonaparte, 'there remains St. Jean d'Acre.' This fortress was the seat of the pasha, Jezzar. It is on the sea-shore, and accordingly England could intervene. Admiral Sir Sidney Smith, commanding a squadron on the coast, opened fire on the French as they approached the shore, and was surprised to find his fire answered only by musketry. In a moment he divined that the siege artillery was to come from Alexandria by sea, and very speedily he discovered and captured the ships that carried it. On March 19 Bonaparte is before Acre, but the place receives supplies from the sea, and support from the English ships, while his artillery is lost. He is detained there for two whole months, and retires at last without success. This check, he said, changed the destiny of the world, for he calculated that the fall of Jezzar would have been followed by the adhesion of all the subject tribes, Druses and Christians, which would have given him an army ready for the conquest of Asia.

The failure had been partially redeemed by a victory won in April over an army which had marched from the interior to the relief of Acre under Abdallah Pasha, and which Bonaparte defeated on the plain of Esdraelon (the battle is usually named from Mount Tabor). In the middle of May the retreat began, a counterpart on a small scale of the retreat from Moscow, heat and pestilence taking the place of frost and the Cossacks. On the 24th he is again at Jaffa, from which he writes his report to the Directory, explaining that he had deliberately abstained from entering Acre because of the plague which, as he heard, was ravaging the city. On June 14 his letters are again dated from Cairo. His second stay in Egypt lasts two months, which were spent partly in hunting the dethroned chief of the Mamelukes, Murad Bey, partly in meeting a new Turkish army, which arrived in July in the Bay of Aboukir. He inflicted on it an annihilating defeat near its landing-place; according to his own account nearly nine thousand persons were drowned. This victory masked the final failure of the expedition. It was a failure such as would have given a serious blow to the reputation even of Bonaparte in a state enjoying publicity, where the responsibility could have been brought home to him and the facts could have been discussed.

For a year of warfare, for the loss of the fleet, of 6,000 soldiers, and of several distinguished officers (Brueys, Caffarelli, Cretin), for disastrous defeats suffered in Europe, which might have been averted by Bonaparte and his army, for the loss for an indefinite time of the army itself, which could only return to France by permission of the English, there was nothing to show. No progress was made in conciliating the people. Bonaparte had arrived with an intention of appealing to the religious instinct of the Semitic races. He had imagined apparently that the rebellion of France against the Catholic Church might be represented to the Moslems as an adhesion to their faith. He had declared himself a Mussulman commissioned by the Most High to humble the Cross. At the same time he had hoped to conciliate the Sultan; it had been arranged that Talleyrand should go to Constantinople for the purpose. But Talleyrand remained at Paris, the Sultan was not conciliated, the people were not deluded by Bonaparte's religious appeals. Rebellion after rebellion had broken out, and had been repressed with savage cruelty. It was time for him to extricate himself from so miserable a business.

It appears from the correspondence that he had promised to be back in France as early as October, 1798, a fact which shows how completely all his calculations had been disappointed. Sir Sidney Smith now contrived that he should receive a packet of journals, by which he was informed of all that had passed recently in Europe and of the disasters which France had suffered. His resolution was immediately taken. On August 22 he wrote to Kléber announcing that he transferred to him the command of the expedition, and that he himself would return to Europe, taking with him Berthier, Lannes, Murat, Andréossi, Marmont, Monge, and Berthollet, and leaving orders that Junot should follow in October and Desaix in November. After carefully spreading false accounts of his intentions, he set sail with two frigates in the night of the 22d. His voyage occupied more than six weeks, during which he revisited Corsica. On October 9 he arrived in the harbor of Fréjus.

After his return the disastrous results of the expedition continued to develop themselves. Egypt was reconquered by the English, and Malta passed into their hands. Thus a plan which had aimed at excluding England from the Mediterranean ended in establishing her power there and in excluding France. We shall see how far Napoleon was ultimately led in the wild struggle to retrieve this failure.

§ 5. *Revolution of Brumaire.*

From this moment the tide of his fortune began to flow again. His reappearance seemed providential, and was hailed with delight throughout France, where the Republican Government was in the last stage of dissolution. Since Fructidor French policy had been systematically warlike. A great law of military service had been introduced by General Jourdan, which was the basis of the Napoleonic armies; a series of violent aggressions in Switzerland and Central Italy had brought on a new European war. But this policy was evidently inconsistent with the republican form of government established in 1795. A Directory of civilians were not qualified to conduct a policy so systematically warlike. Hence the war of 1799 had been palpably mismanaged. The armies and the generals were there, but the presiding strategist and statesman was wanting. In Italy conquest had been pushed too far. Half the troops were locked up in fortresses, or occupied in suppressing rebellions; hence Macdonald at the Trebbia and Joubert at Novi were defeated by Suwaroff, Mantua fell, and the work of Bonaparte in Italy was wellnigh undone. Government was shaken by these disasters. A kind of revolution took place in June. Four new members entered the Directory, of whom three — Gohier, Roger-Ducos, and General Moulins — represented on the whole the revival of the Jacobinism of 1793, while the fourth, Sieyès, the most important politician of this crisis, represented the desire for some new constitutional experiment. The remedy which first suggested itself was to return to the warlike fury and terrorism of 1793. The Jacobin Club was revived, and held its sittings in the Salle du Manège. Many leading generals, especially Jourdan and Bernadotte, favored it. But 1793 was not to be revived. Its passions had gone to sleep, and the memory of it was a nightmare. Nevertheless a sort of Terror began. The hardship of recruitment caused rebellions, particularly in the West. Chouannerie and royalism revived, and the odious Law of Hostages was passed to check them. After seven years of misery France in the autumn of 1799 was perhaps more miserable than ever.

If 1793 could not be revived, what alternative? Sieyès perceived that what was needed was a supreme general to direct the war. But, though he had ceased to believe in popular institutions, and had become a convert to a new kind of aristocracy, he did not wish his supreme general to control civil affairs. He looked for an officer who should be intelligent without being too ambitious. His choice fell upon Joubert, who was accordingly nominated commander of the Army of Italy, that he might acquire the necessary renown. But Joubert was killed at Novi in August. From this time Sieyès had remained uncertain. Advances were made in vain to Moreau. Who can say what might have happened in a few months? Some general of abilities not very commanding would have risen to a position in which he would have controlled the fate of France. Perhaps Masséna, whose reputation at this moment reached its highest point through the victories of Zurich, but who was not made either for an emperor or for a statesman, might have come forward to play the part of Monk.

Upon this perplexing gloom the reappearance of Bonaparte came like a tropical sunrise, too dazzling for Sieyès himself, who wanted a general, but a general he could control. On October 16 he arrived at his old Parisian house in the Rue de la Victoire, and on November 9 and 10 (Brumaire 18, 19) the revolution took place. Bonaparte had some difficulty at first in understanding the position. He found a Jacobin party clamoring for strong measures and for a vigorous prosecution of the war; at the head of this party he saw military men, particularly Jourdan and Bernadotte. As an old Robespierrist, a Fructidorian, and a soldier, he was at first attracted to this faction. Sieyès, the object of their most bitter attacks, he was at first disposed to regard as his principal enemy. Gradually he came to perceive that this time he was to rise not as a Jacobin but as the soldier of anti-Jacobinism, and that he must place his sword at the service of Sieyès. For his part Sieyès could not but perceive that Bonaparte was not precisely the war-minister he sought. But by the efforts of Lucien and Joseph Bonaparte, of Roederer, and Talleyrand, a coalition was at last effected between them, though Sieyès continued to predict that after the success Bonaparte would throw him over. The movement which now took place was the most respectable, the most hopeful, as for a long time it seemed the most successful, effort that had been made since 1792 to lift France out of the slough. Instead of reviving Jacobinism the proposal was to organize a strong and skilled Government. A grand party of respectability rallied round Sieyès to put down Jacobinism. Ducos among the Directors (he had been converted), the majority of the Council of Ancients, Moreau and Macdonald, the generals of purest reputation, Bonaparte and the generals personally attached to him, composed this party. On the other side the Jacobinical party consisted of the Directors Gohier and Moulins, the majority of the Council of Five

Hundred, Generals Jourdan and Bernadotte. Which party would be followed by the rank and file of the army, was an anxious question.

It was determined to take advantage of a provision of the constitution which had been originally inserted by the Girondists as a safeguard against aggressions from the municipality of Paris, and to cause the Council of Ancients to decree a meeting of the Councils outside Paris at the palace of St. Cloud. At this meeting it was intended to propose a reform of the constitution. The proposal would be supported by a majority in the Council of Ancients, and by many, but probably not a majority, in the Council of Five Hundred. It was foreseen that the Jacobins might give trouble, and might need to be eliminated, as they had themselves eliminated the Girondists. With a view to this, when the decree was passed on November 9, General Bonaparte, made commander of all the troops in Paris, was intrusted with the execution of it. It is carefully to be observed that he does not, like Cromwell, act of his own free will against the assembly, but is appointed by the assembly to act in its name. No one thought of destroying the republic; the question was of introducing the famous perfect constitution of Sieyès. Bonaparte appeared, surrounded by the generals of his party, in the Council of Ancients, where he skilfully evaded taking the oath to the constitution. He then reviewed the troops, and it became apparent that he could count on them. From this moment Brumaire may be said to have been decided. The next step was that Sieyès and Ducos resigned their places on the Directory; Barras was induced to follow their example; but Gohier and Moulins were firm. Gohier was placed under ward of Moreau at the Luxembourg, while Moulins made his escape. It now only remained to deal with the Council of Five Hundred, the stronghold of Jacobinism.

The revolution was consummated on the next day at St. Cloud. Bonaparte and Sieyès sat in a private room while the Councils began their deliberations; but being informed that it was proposed to renew the oath to the existing constitution, Bonaparte determined to interfere. There seems to have been mismanagement here. Sieyès, not Bonaparte, should have interfered, but probably he was rendered helpless, as often happened to him, by timidity. Bonaparte then entered the Council of Ancients, where he delivered a confused harangue, which did him little good, though the assembly was well disposed to him. His position was a false one, though he urged very justly that the existing constitution had been practically destroyed by the illegalities of Fructidor, Floréal, and Prairial. He then passed to the hostile Council of Five Hundred, where he was received with cries of 'Hors la loi!' 'A bas le dictateur!' He was seized by the collar, and attempts were made to push him out of the hall.

He was now almost in despair, and no wonder! By the backwardness of Sieyès he had been pushed into the part of Cromwell. But Cromwell had soldiers devoted to him, and of theocratic rather than republican ideas; the soldiers of Bonaparte had only just been put under his command, and they were fanatical republicans. The false step must be retrieved. The soldiers must be persuaded that Bonaparte was no Cromwell, but a staunch republican, and that they were not called upon to act against an assembly, but only against a traitorous minority, as at Fructidor. Lucien Bonaparte, who was president of the Five Hundred, performed this miracle. Bonaparte had sent grenadiers to rescue him. Lucien was at the tribune, where he was defending his brother amidst noisy interruption. At the appearance of the grenadiers he threw off his official dress and retired under their escort. In the hall he mounted on horseback and addressed the troops who were employed to guard the legislature, declaring that the council was oppressed by assassins, brigands paid by England; he charged the soldiers to deliver the majority from this oppression by clearing the hall. He brandished a sword and swore to stab his brother if ever he attacked the liberties of Frenchmen. On the clear understanding that no violence against the assembly was intended, and with the express sanction of its president, the soldiers then cleared the hall. In the evening at 9 o'clock Lucien reassembled a certain number of the members and proposed to them to nominate a committee which should report on the state of affairs. This committee was at once named, and speedily presented a report to the effect that Sieyès, Roger-Ducos, and Bonaparte should compose a provisional executive under the title of consuls, that the legislature should adjourn till February 20 (1 Ventose), a committee of twenty-five members from each Council being left to deliberate along with the consuls upon the changes to be made in the constitution; at the same time, as in Fructidor, a certain number of members (fifty-five) were to be expelled from the Councils.

Thus the original plan was on the whole carried into effect. But it had been sadly marred by

the unseemly appearance of Bonaparte and by his
gasconades, in which he bade the Council remember that he 'marched under the escort of the god
of fortune and the god of war.' An attempt was
made to conceal these mistakes by publishing in
the *Moniteur* a garbled report of his speech.

CHAPTER III.

THE FIRST CONSUL.

§ 1. *Bonaparte becomes First Consul.*

BRUMAIRE taken by itself is the victory of Sieyès rather than of Bonaparte. It raised Sieyès to the position he had so long coveted of legislator for France. The constitution now introduced was really in great part his work, but his work so signally altered in one point that it resulted in the absolute supremacy of Bonaparte. We should especially notice that it is Sieyès, not Bonaparte, who practically suppresses representative institutions. The long-expected scheme of Sieyès was at last promulgated, and we see with astonishment that the man of 1789, the author of 'Qu'est-ce que le Tiers-Etat?' himself condemns political liberty. In this scheme the assemblies, of which there are three, the Senate, the Tribunate, and the Corps Législatif, are not chosen by popular election at all. The two latter are nominated by the Senate, and the Senate is chosen at the outset in part by

the provisional consuls and in part by co-optation.
The Tribunate alone has the right of public debate,
which is separated from the right of voting. This
latter is assigned to the Corps Législatif. These
arrangements, which caused the nullity of parliamentary institutions in the Napoleonic period,
were devised not by Bonaparte but by Sieyès, who
confined popular election to certain lists of notabil-
ity, out of which the assemblies were required to
be chosen. By this scheme Sieyès, who retained
all his hatred for the old *régime* and the old *noblesse*, passed sentence upon the whole constructive
work of the Revolution; this sentence was but ratified by Bonaparte.

But, while he absolutely condemned democracy,
Sieyès did not want to set up despotism. The
Senate was to be supreme; it was to be a kind of
hereditary aristocracy, the depositary of the tradition of the Revolution; above it, and capable of
being deposed by it, was to be a doge called Grand
Elector, whose main function would consist in
choosing two consuls, of whom one was to take the
home and the other the foreign department. Here
again Bonaparte acquiesced as far as he could. He
adopted the consuls and the triple executive, even
lowering apparently the Grand Elector of Sieyès
by giving him the more republican title of First

Consul. But he displayed signally the adroitness, rapid and audacious, which was always the characteristic of his diplomacy. He declaimed violently against the feebleness of the Grand Elector and the Consuls in this scheme, feigning to overlook that it concentrated power intentionally in the Senate; then, instead of sending back the scheme for revision, he simply strengthened immensely the attributions of the First Consul, leaving the other consuls and the assemblies as weak as before. By this stroke a strong aristocracy was turned into a strong monarchy; at the same time advantage was taken of the very peculiar character of Sieyès, who always when he met with opposition sank into an impenetrable silence. Bonaparte boasted afterwards that he had sealed his victory over Sieyès by a handsome bribe at the expense of the public.

Perhaps, however, in his controversy with Sieyès Bonaparte had public opinion on his side. Not only were the arrangements he attacked really absurd, but he might just at that moment plead for a strong government without being instantly found guilty of ambition. The conviction of the time was that a strong and stable executive was needed, and that this must not be many-headed; moreover the discovery had recently been made in

America that a Republic must have a President, and also that such a President might be without ambition.

The provisional consulate of Sieyès, Ducos, and Bonaparte lasted only from November 10 to December 13. Then through the promulgation of the new constitution it made way for the definitive consulate of Bonaparte, Cambacérès, and Lebrun, which lasted four years. By the constitution of 22 Frimaire, year VIII. (which was never debated in any assembly, but, after being devised by the two legislative committees meeting at the Luxembourg under the presidency of Bonaparte, and in the presence of the other consuls, and after being redacted by Daunou, was introduced by a popular vote), Bonaparte became First Consul for ten years with a salary of half a million francs, with a sole power of nominating the council of state, the ministers, ambassadors, officers of army and fleet, and most of the judges and local officials, and with a power, in nominal conjunction with the other consuls, of initiating all legislation and deciding war and peace. Sieyès and Ducos retired, and under the new constitution the second and third consuls were Cambacérès, an eminent legist, and Lebrun, an old official of Louis XV.'s time. The party of Brumaire had intended to set up a republic, but this constitution created a strong monarchy under the thinnest disguise.

For the moment it was much that France renounced Jacobinism and ceased to tear herself to pieces. The civil war of the West and the foreign war were alike energetically taken in hand. A proclamation to the inhabitants of the West (December 28) breathed for the first time the spirit of tolerance, of respect for religion, and consideration for the clergy. It was a precursor of the Concordat, and attacked the civil war at its root. It was accompanied by the most imperious threats against the refractory, who are to be treated 'like the Arabs of the desert,' who are warned that they have to do with a man 'accustomed to rigorous and energetic measures'— an allusion apparently to the massacres of Jaffa and Cairo. This policy, accompanied by decisive military action, was speedily successful. By the end of February all was quiet in the West; Frotté, the most active leader in Normandy, had surrendered at discretion, and had been shot, though Bonaparte had expressly announced that if he surrendered he might count on the generosity of the Government. In preaching a religious peace at home Bonaparte was sincere; he was less so in announcing a policy of peace in Europe, for he well knew that he needed a victory to cover his apostasy. Nevertheless the announcement was necessary as part of the national renunciation of Jacobinism; and it was harmless, for the Coalition was scarcely likely to accept peace when they had the military advantage. Indeed they could not consistently do so, since they had gone to war on the ground that peace with the Directory had appeared in 1798 to be less endurable than war, and the accession of Bonaparte could not but seem to them likely to make matters worse. In thinking thus they were substantially right, as the sequel proved, but they did not sufficiently understand that Bonaparte was not now the 'champion of Jacobinism,' as Pitt called him, but had become its enemy and destroyer. When England and Austria refused his overtures, Bonaparte had the satisfaction of getting precisely what he wanted — viz. war — in precisely the way he wished, that is, as apparently forced upon him.

§ 2. *His Jealousy of Moreau. — Campaign of Marengo. — Treaty of Lunéville. — The Concordat. — Treaty of Amiens.*

The campaign of 1800 is peculiar in the circumstance that throughout its course Bonaparte has a military rival with whom he is afraid to break, and who keeps pace with him in achievements —

Moreau. To Moreau the success of Brumaire had been mainly due, and he had perhaps thought that the new constitution, as it did not seem to contemplate the First Consul commanding an army, had removed Bonaparte from the path of his ambition. He now held the command of the principal army, that of the Rhine, in which post Bonaparte could not venture to supersede him. The problem for Bonaparte throughout the war was to prevent Moreau, and in a less degree Masséna, who was now in command of the Army of Italy, from eclipsing his own military reputation. Russia had now retired from the Coalition, so that, as in 1796, Austria and England were the only belligerents. Italy had been almost entirely lost, and Masséna, at the head of the Army of Italy, opposed to General Melas, was almost where Bonaparte had been before his Italian campaign began. But France had retained the control of Switzerland, and Moreau, with more than 100,000 men arranged along the Rhine from the Lake of Constance to Alsace, stood opposed to Kray, whose head-quarters were at Donaueschingen. It seemed that the campaign would be conducted by Moreau and Masséna receiving instructions from Bonaparte at Paris. That the decisive campaign would have been in Bavaria, seems so evident that the military writer Bülow conjectures that the French were afraid of alarming Europe by a too decisive victory, which would have brought them at once to the walls of Vienna, and that they therefore transferred the campaign to Italy. But Bonaparte would have sunk into a President had Moreau won Hohenlinden in the spring of 1800, while he remained ingloriously at Paris. While therefore in writing to Moreau he carefully adopts the language of one who, much to his own regret, has become a mere civilian, he plans the campaign so that both Moreau and Masséna are confined to the task of holding the enemy in play, while an army of reserve descends from one of the Alpine passes into Italy. This army of reserve, which was so carefully concealed that few people believed in its existence, is to be commanded, he writes, by some general 'to be named by the consuls;' a little later Berthier is nominated. As late as the end of March he told Miot that he did not mean to leave Paris. Moreau is also to detach 25,000 men under Lecourbe, who are to join Berthier in Italy; in this way security was taken that Moreau should not be too successful. On April 24 the campaign in Germany began by the passage of the Rhine at a number of points at once. Up to May 10 Moreau is the hero of the war. He is victorious at Engen, at Mösskirchen, and forces Kray to retire to Ulm. By those successes Switzerland is kept clear for the operations of Bonaparte. On May 9 Bonaparte is at Geneva, and it appears at once that he is commander, and Berthier only his chief of the staff. At the same time Carnot in person is sent with unusual formality to demand from Moreau the detachment of troops.

The campaign of Marengo was astonishingly short. On May 11 Bonaparte left Geneva, and he is in Paris again early in July. Since the beginning of April Masséna had been struggling vainly against the superior forces of Melas. Since the 21st he had been shut up in Genoa, where Austria and England could co-operate in the siege. In Italy the affairs of France looked darker than ever, when Bonaparte threw himself on the rear of Melas by passing the Great St. Bernard between May 15 and 20. Other divisions passed the Little St. Bernard and the Mont Cenis, while the detachment from Moreau's army (under Moncey, not Lecourbe) descended the St. Gotthard. It seems that the Austrians had absolutely refused to believe, what nevertheless was openly discussed in the Paris journals, that Bonaparte intended to cross the Alps. Bonaparte had another surprise in store for them. Though Genoa was now suffering all the horrors of famine, he made no attempt to relieve it, but turned to the left, entered Milan on June 2, and took possession of the whole line of the Ticino and the Po. Meanwhile Genoa capitulated to General Ott. Melas was now at Alessandria, where Bonaparte sought him on the 13th. On the 14th Melas marched out, crossed the Bormida, and arrived at Marengo. He found the French widely dispersed, and fairly defeated them. He had himself retired from the field, and his soldiers were plundering the dead, when the arrival of Desaix's division gave Bonaparte a gleam of hope. Desaix himself fell, but a sudden charge of cavalry, headed by Kellermann, produced among the Austrians a panic similar to that which had been witnessed at Rivoli. A great Austrian victory was turned into a decisive Austrian defeat. Bonaparte was raised from the brink of absolute ignominious ruin to the very pinnacle of glory. On the next day Melas (having, as it seems quite lost his head) signed a convention by which Austria sacrificed almost all North Italy, restoring something like the position of Campo Formio. 'Had he fought another battle,' says Marmont, 'he would certainly have beaten us.' Bonaparte returns to Paris, victorious at once over Austria and over Moreau and Masséna. He did not, however, succeed in tearing from Moreau the honor of concluding the war. Marengo did not lead to peace; this was won, where naturally it could only be won, in Bavaria by Moreau's victory of Hohenlinden (December 3), a victory perhaps greater than any of which at that time Bonaparte could boast.

This campaign is the culmination and close of what may be called the Bonaparte period, the period of war on a comparatively small scale and of victories won with small means. It exaggerates all the characteristics of Bonaparte's method — startling originality, cunning, and audacity. Genius is prodigally displayed, and yet an immense margin is left for fortune. Marengo may be called his crowning victory. The position given him by the new constitution had hitherto been most precarious. Sieyès and the republicans were on the watch for him on the one side; Moreau seemed on the point of eclipsing him on the other. His family felt their critical position: 'had he fallen at Marengo,' writes Lucien, 'we should have been all proscribed.' Perhaps nothing but a stroke so rapid and startling as that of Marengo could have saved him from these difficulties. But this did more, and developed the empire out of the consulate.

His appeal for peace after Brumaire had not been purely insincere, though he wanted victory before peace. He proposes to Rouget de l' Isle to write 'a battle hymn which shall express the idea that with great nations peace comes after victory.' After Marengo he devotes himself to giving peace to the world; he did this by three great acts, so that in 1802 for the first time for ten years under the new Augustus 'no war or battle sound was heard the world around.' These three acts are the treaty of Lunéville, February, 1801, the Concordat, July, 1801, the treaty of Amiens, March, 1802. It is worth noticing that the negotiator of all of them is his brother Joseph, as if he especially desired to connect his family name with the pacification of the world.

1. The treaty of Lunéville gave peace to the Continent. Austria is now disarmed, not merely by defeat, but still more by the defection of Russia to the side of France. It is to be observed that here Bonaparte shows himself at least less rapacious than the Directory. He surrenders most of the usurpations of 1798, the Roman and Parthenopean republics, and returns in the main to the arrangements of Campo Formio — a proof of moderation which must have led the cabinets to consider whether after all it might not be possible to

find a *modus vivendi* with the Government of Brumaire.

2. By the Concordat he professed to close the religious war. In reality he crushed the national Gallican Church, which had been created by the Constitution Civile, and which had perhaps begun to take root, and restored the Papal Church, shorn of its endowments and dependent, so long as he lived, on the state. As part of the great pacification, the Concordat was perhaps mainly a stroke of stage effect, though its influence upon the later history of France has been great. For Bonaparte himself it was important as severing the clerical party from the Bourbons and attaching it to himself, as giving him through the clergy an influence over the peasantry, upon whom he depended for his armies, also as in some degree welding together through the ubiquitous influence of the clergy the different states which were already subject to his government. In negotiating it with Cardinal Consalvi, Bonaparte had recourse more than once to the vulgar fraud and knavery which earned for him the title of Jupiter-Scapin.

3. It remained to make peace with England, but here the condition of peace, victory, was still wanting. For a moment, however, it seemed within reach, for the Czar had gone over to France, and

had become bitterly hostile to England. This opened quite a new prospect. It enabled Bonaparte to revive against England the Armed Neutrality of 1780. Not only Russia but Prussia was thus brought for the first time, along with Sweden and Denmark, into the French alliance, and the system of Tilsit was sketched out. But this phase lasted only till April. The bombardment of Copenhagen by Nelson dissolved the combination, and the murder of Paul, followed by a reconciliation between Russia and England, compelled Bonaparte to lower his pretensions. In the summer his endeavors are confined to saving the French colony in Egypt from the English, and to snatching a little territory from England's ally Portugal by means of Spain. But Cairo capitulated to the English in June, in which month also Spain made peace with Portugal. Bonaparte was at last compelled to admit in this instance the idea of a peace which should not come after victory. Accordingly, in October, the preliminaries of London were signed, and the treaty of Amiens followed in March. The allies of France paid for her naval defeats, Spain losing Trinidad and Holland Ceylon; but France, though she lost nothing, acquiesced by this treaty in the total failure of all her designs upon the East.

§ 3. *Reconstruction of French Institutions.* — *Gradual Progress towards Monarchy.* — *Plot of Nivose.*

The globe was now at peace, and thanked Bonaparte for it. The equilibrium which had been destroyed by the Revolution seemed at length to be restored. Meanwhile the legislative reconstruction of France proceeded rapidly. This is the glorious period of Bonaparte's life, not, as has often been alleged, because he was as yet uncorrupted by power, but simply because a strong intelligent Government was the great need of France and repose the great need of Europe, and Bonaparte at this time satisfied both needs. The work of reconstruction which distinguishes the consulate, though it was continued under the empire, is the most enduring of all the achievements of Napoleon. The institutions of modern France date, not, as is often said, from the Revolution, but from the Consulate. Not that Napoleon personally was endowed with a supreme legislative genius; his principal merit was to have given to France the first secure Government, the first Government capable of effective legislation, that she had had since the destruction of her ancient institutions. The task of reconstruction fell to him of necessity; his personal interference was in many

respects, as we shall see, mischievous rather than
beneficial; it is, however, also true that he appreciated the greatness of the work, urged it on with
vigor, entered into it, impressed it with the stamp
of his own personality, and left upon it the traces
of his keen sagacity.

The institutions now created, and which form
the organisation of modern France, are — (1) the
restored Church, resting on the Concordat; (2) the
University, resting on the law of 11 Floréal, An
X. (May 1, 1802); (3) the judicial system, commenced by the law of 27 Ventose, An VIII.
(March 18, 1800), and completed by other laws
in 1810; (4) the Codes : — (a) Code Civil (commission nominated 24 Thermidor, An VIII,
August 12, 1800; it received the name Code
Napoléon on September 3, 1807), (b) Code de
Commerce (promulgated on September 10, 1807),
(c) Code Penal, (d) Code d'Instruction Criminelle
(came into force January 1, 1811); (5) the system
of local government, resting on the law of 18
Pluviose, An VIII. (February 7, 1800); (6) the
Bank of France, established 28 Nivose, An VIII.
(January 18, 1800); (7) the Legion of Honor,
established 29 Floréal, An X. (May 19, 1802).
These institutions, along with the military system,
have in the main continued to the present day after

the downfall of all the Napoleonic institutions which were purely political. It is rather the fortune than the merit of Napoleon that no similar mass of legislation can be ascribed to any other sovereign, since no other sovereign has ruled securely over an ancient and civilized country which has been suddenly deprived of all its institutions. It is also a matter of course that much of this legislation has been beneficial, since a *tabula rasa* relieves the legislator of many hindrances. In several points, on the other hand, we can see that France was sacrificed to Napoleon's personal interest. Thus the Concordat restored the ancient Papal Church, shorn of its wealth, and receiving from the state a subsidy of about £2,000,000. It was right to restore religion, and the Constitution Civile, which was cancelled by the Concordat, had been an insane act, the principal cause of the miseries of France for ten years. Nevertheless a great opportunity was lost of trying some new experiment, which might have led to a genuine revival of religion; but for this Napoleon cared nothing so long as he could pose as a new Constantine, detach the Church from the cause of the Bourbons, and have the Pope at his beck. In like manner the freedom of local government was sacrificed to the exigencies of his despotism. Among the most remarkable of his institutions was the University. The twenty-one universities of old France, including the great mother university of Paris, had fallen in the Revolution along with the Church; nothing of the least efficiency had been established in their place, so that in March, 1800, Lucien Bonaparte could write, 'Since the suppression of the teaching corporations instruction has almost ceased to exist in France.' By laws of May, 1806, and March, 1808, was founded the modern University— that is, the whole teaching profession formed into a corporation and endowed by the state, a kind of church of education. This remarkable institution still exists. It has far too much centralization, and is in no way equal to the old system when that is intelligently worked, as in Germany; many learned men have severely condemned it; still it was an important constructive effort, and gave Napoleon the occasion for some striking and original remarks.

From the time of the battle of Marengo the system of Brumaire began to take a development which perhaps had not been clearly foreseen. Sieyès had wished to confine Bonaparte to the War Department, Moreau perhaps had wished to keep him at Paris; in either case it had not been intended to create an august monarchy. But the fabulous success of Marengo, joined to the proofs Bonaparte gave of a really superior intelligence and commanding character, turned the French mind back into that monarchical groove in which it had so long run before the Revolution. Popular liberty had been already renounced by Sieyès, and the disastrous failure of republican institutions, which in four years, from 1795 to 1799, had brought the country to bankruptcy, civil war, and almost barbarism, inclined all public men to agree with him. The choice then could only lie between some form of aristocracy and the revival of monarchy either in the Bourbon family or in another. Napoleon's personal character decided this question. By the Concordat he wrested from the Bourbons the support of the Church; by his military glory he seduced the *noblesse*, as is seen in the case of Ségur; by the pacification of the world he half reconciled to himself the foreign cabinets. But no sooner did this new form of monarchy begin to appear than Bonaparte found himself surrounded by new dangers. He was exposed to the hatred of the republicans, who had hitherto been appeased by the title of consul, and were now thrown into coalition with the defeated Jacobins, and also to the despair of the royalists, who saw themselves disappointed of restoration at the moment of the failure of republicanism. Nearer his person at the same time court parties began to spring up. His brothers and sisters with Corsican shamelessness began to claim their share in the spoils. While he doubted what form his monarchy should take, and whether some character greater and more unique than that of a hereditary king could not be invented, they urged the claims of the *family.* Thus arose a standing feud between the Bonapartes and the Beauharnais, who in the interest of Josephine, already dreading divorce for her childlessness, opposed the principle of heredity.

In grappling with the defeated parties Bonaparte found a great advantage in his position. The constitution of Brumaire itself gave him great powers; popular institutions had been destroyed, not by him, but by the nation itself, which was weary of them; under the Directory the public had grown accustomed to the suppression of journals and to periodic *coups d' état* of the most savage violence. Bonaparte therefore could establish a rigorous despotism under the forms of a consular republic, mutilate the assemblies, and silence public opinion, he could venture occasionally upon acts of the most sweeping tyranny, without shocking a people which had so lately seen Fructidor, not to say the Reign of Terror, and had been accustomed to call them liberty. The conspiracies began immediately after the return from Marengo, when the Corsicans Arena and Ceracchi, guilty apparently of little more than wild talk, were arrested in October, 1800, at the Théâtre Français. But on December 24 of the same year, as he drove with Josephine to the opera, a sudden explosion took place in the Rue Saint-Nicaise, which killed and wounded several people and damaged about fifty houses; the carriage of Bonaparte escaped. He was still in the first fervor of his conversion from Jacobinism, and had not yet become alive to the danger which threatened him from royalism. He could therefore see nothing but Jacobinism in this plot, and proposed to meet the danger by some general measure calculated to eradicate what remained of the Jacobin party. But before such a measure could be taken Fouché convinced him that he had been in error, and that he was in the presence of a new enemy, royalism roused into new vigor by the recent change in public opinion. Upon this Bonaparte acted most characteristically. By a singular stretch of Machiavelism he made use of the mistake into which he had himself led the public to crush the enemy which for the moment he feared most. He arrested and transported one hundred and thirty persons, whom he knew to be innocent of the plot, on the general ground of Jacobinism, substituting for all legal trial a resolution passed by the servile Senate to the effect that 'the measure was conservative of the constitution.' This is Nivose, an act as enormous as Fructidor, and with a perfidy of its own.

Making use of victory was almost more Bonaparte's talent than winning it. These plots, so far from impeding his ascent to monarchy, were converted by him into steps upon which he mounted. He drew from them an argument for heredity, which, in case he should himself fall, would furnish a successor. It had already been argued in the 'Parallèle entre César, Cromwell, et Bonaparte' (October, 1800) that heredity only could prevent the nation from falling again under the domination of the assemblies, under the yoke of the S (not Sieyès surely, but Soldats) or under that of the Bourbons. He also made the plot of Nivose the occasion of a constitutional innovation. The assemblies devised by Sieyès had hitherto been simply useless, so much idle machinery. But in Nivose the precedent was set of giving the Senate a constituent power. To guard the constitution was its nominal function; this was now converted into a function of sanctioning alterations in the constitution, since every innovation became legal when the Senate declared it to be conservative of the constitution. In the hands of Bonaparte such a principle soon became fruitful enough.

The first open step towards monarchy was made at the conclusion of the treaty of Amiens. As pacificator of the globe it was declared in the tribunate that Bonaparte deserved some mark of public gratitude. Upon this the Senate proposed to re-elect him First Consul for a further term of ten years. Bonaparte, disappointed, declared that he could only owe a prorogation of his magistracy to the people; to them, therefore, the question was referred, but in the form, Shall Napoleon Bonaparte be elected consul for life? and in this form it was adopted.

§ 4. *Rupture with England. — Execution of the Duc d'Enghien. — The Emperor Napoleon. — Trial of Moreau.*

In 1803 it might be perceived that the French Revolution was over; Jacobinism was dead, the Church was restored, and it was plain that Bonaparte did not mean to be the first president of a republic, but the restorer of monarchy. The new monarchy was seen to be similar to the old, but considerably more imperious. France is covered with an army of functionaries, servilely dependent on the Government; a strange silence has settled on the country which under the old *régime* had been noisy with the debate — if for the most part fruitless debate — of parliaments and estates. Europe might hope that, the volcano being exhausted, she would henceforth be free from war. With Jacobinism the source of discord was removed. All depended on Bonaparte himself, who might be supposed to be satiated with military glory, and to have enough to occupy him in the reconstitution of French Government and society.

Alas! the new age, as it defined itself in 1803, proved even more terribly warlike than the age of unexampled discord which had just closed.

France, indeed, had been left most dangerously strong, and yet it was not simply lust of conquest in Bonaparte that now darkened the face of affairs, it was the rivalry of England and France breaking out more fiercely than at any earlier epoch. The crisis was such as to give this old rivalry a sharper edge than ever. It was unendurable for Bonaparte in his glory to submit to the total failure of his Egyptian scheme; on the other hand, England was obliged, considering the immense and threatening ascendency of France in Europe, to cling convulsively to every advantage she had gained. Everything turned on Malta, that all-important position, which England might have surrendered to some neutral occupancy had Bonaparte been less powerful and dangerous; and yet it was gall and wormwood to Bonaparte to imagine his darling conquest remaining in English hands. He had rather, he said, see the English in the Faubourg St. Antoine than in Malta. This rupture between England and France is the beginning of the Napoleonic age, and determines its whole character.

It is somewhat difficult to understand, because in the eleven years of the war with England Bonaparte was never able to strike a single blow at his enemy, and because at the outset he candidly confessed to Lord Whitworth that he did not see what means he had of injuring England. Why did Bonaparte engage in a war in which he was condemned to be so purely passive? We are perhaps to suppose that his confidence in the favor of fortune had been vastly increased by his recent successes, particularly by Marengo, and that though to Lord Whitworth he spoke of the invasion of England as almost impossible, yet in reality he expected to achieve that impossibility, as he had achieved so many others. He had also in mind the indirect methods which he afterwards employed; he would use, if necessary, the fleets of other Powers, he would resort to the commercial blockade; in one way or another he felt certain of success. That he was really bent upon forcing a war appears from his allowing Sébastiani's report of his mission in the East, full of hints of the intention of France to reoccupy Egypt at the first opportunity, to appear in the *Moniteur*. This report, besides offending England, caused her to keep resolute possession of Malta, and, when Bonaparte appealed to the treaty of Amiens, England replied by pointing to the new annexations of France, which had just divided Piedmont into departments. 'Ce sont des bagatelles,' Lord Whitworth reports Bonaparte to have answered, but he adds in a parenthesis which has never been printed, 'The expression he made use of was too trivial and vulgar to find a place in a despatch, or anywhere but in the mouth of a hackney coachman!'

The rupture took place with extraordinary marks of irritation on the part of Bonaparte. He detained the English residents in France, he declared that he would hear of no neutrality, and indeed the continental wars which followed, in the course of which the Napoleonic Empire was founded, had their origin mainly in this quarrel. It might perhaps have been expected that he would try to conciliate the continental Powers until he should have settled accounts with England. But he thought himself able to summon them to his side and to make them enemies of England against their will. Indeed since Lunéville he felt himself the master of Germany. By that settlement Austria had lost her power within the empire, and the minor German princes now looked up to Napoleon, for Napoleon dispensed the mass of property, the plunder of bishoprics and townships, which had been decreed as indemnity to the princes dispossessed on the left bank of the Rhine. Hence he does not hesitate after the rupture with England to take up a position in the heart of Germany by seizing Hanover.

All this was done while Bonaparte was still nominally only consul in the French Republic. But the rupture with England furnished him with the occasion of throwing off the last disguise and openly restoring monarchy. It was a step which required all his audacity and cunning. He had crushed Jacobinism, but two great parties remained. There was first the more moderate republicanism, which might be called Girondism, and was widely spread among all classes and particularly in the army. Secondly, there was the old royalism, which after many years of helpless weakness had revived since Brumaire. These two parties, though hostile to each other, were forced into a sort of alliance by the new attitude of Bonaparte, who was hurrying France at once into a new revolution at home and into an abyss of war abroad. England too, after the rupture, favored the efforts of these parties. Royalism from England began to open communications with moderate republicanism in France. Pichegru acted for the former, and the great representative of the latter was Moreau, who had helped to make Brumaire in the tacit expectation probably of rising to the consulate in due course when Bonaparte's term should have expired, and was therefore hurt in his personal claims as well as in his republican principles. Bonaparte watched the movement through his ubiquitous police, and with characteristic strategy determined not merely to defeat it but to make it his stepping-stone to monarchy. He would ruin Moreau by fastening on him the stigma of royalism; he would persuade France to make him emperor in order to keep out the Bourbons. He achieved this with the peculiar mastery which he always showed in villanous intrigue. Moreau had in 1797 incurred blame by concealing his knowledge of Pichegru's dealings with the royalists. That he should now meet and hold

conversation with Pichegru at a moment when
Pichegru was engaged in contriving a royalist rebellion, associated his name still more closely with
royalism, and Pichegru brought with him wilder
partisans, such as Georges the Chouan. No doubt
Moreau would gladly have seen and gladly have
helped an insurrection against Bonaparte; any
republican, and, what is more, any patriot, would
at that moment have risked much to save France
from the ruin that Bonaparte was bringing on her.
But Bonaparte succeeded in associating him with
royalist schemes and with schemes of assassination. Controlling the Senate, he was able to
suppress the jury; controlling every avenue of
publicity, he was able to suppress opinion; and
the army, Moreau's fortress, was won through its
hatred of royalism. In this way Bonaparte's last
personal rival was removed. There remained the
royalists, and Bonaparte hoped to seize their leader,
the Comte d'Artois, who was expected, as the
police knew, soon to join Pichegru and Georges
at Paris. What Bonaparte would have done with
him we may judge from the course he took when
the Comte did not come. On March 15, 1804,
the Duc d'Enghien, grandson of the Prince de
Condé, residing at Ettenheim in Baden, was seized
at midnight by a party of dragoons, brought to

Paris, where he arrived on the 20th, confined in the castle of Vincennes, brought before a military commission at two o'clock the next morning, asked whether he had not borne arms against the republic, which he acknowledged himself to have done, conducted to a staircase above the moat, and there shot and buried in the moat.

This deed was perfectly consistent with Bonaparte's professed principles, so that no misunderstanding or passing fit of passion is required to explain it. He had made, shortly before, a formal offer to the pretender through the king of Prussia, by which he had undertaken to pay him a handsome pension in return for the formal abdication of his rights. This had been refused, and Bonaparte felt free. That the best course was to strike at the heads of the family was a shrewd conclusion. Neither Louis nor Charles were precisely heroes; and then the whole revolutionary party in France would applaud a new tragedy like that of January, 1793. Accordingly Bernadotte and Curée were delighted with it. That the Duc d'Enghien was innocent of the conspiracy, was nothing to the purpose; the act was political, not judicial; accordingly he was not even charged with complicity. That the execution would strike horror into the cabinets, and perhaps bring about a new Coalition, belonged to a class of considerations which at this time Bonaparte systematically disregarded.

This affair led immediately to the thought of giving heredity to Bonaparte's power. The thought seems to have commended itself irresistibly even to strong republicans and to those who were most shocked by the murder. To make Bonaparte's position more secure seemed the only way of averting a new Reign of Terror or new convulsions. He himself felt some embarrassment. Like Cromwell, he was afraid of the republicanism of the army, and heredity pure and simple brought him face to face with the question of divorcing Josephine. To propitiate the army he chose from the titles suggested to him — consul, stadtholder, &c. — that of emperor, undoubtedly the most accurate, and having a sufficiently military sound. The other difficulty, after much furious dissension between the two families of Bonaparte and Beauharnais, was evaded by giving Napoleon himself (but none of his successors) a power of adoption, and fixing the succession, in default of a direct heir natural or adoptive, first in Joseph and his descendants, then in Louis and his descendants. Except abstaining from the regal title, no attempt was made to conceal the abolition of republicanism.

Bonaparte was to be called Napoleon, and 'sire' and 'majesté;' grand dignitaries with grand titles were appointed, the second and third consuls becoming now arch-chancellor and arch-treasurer respectively; and 'citoyen' from this time gave way to 'monsieur.' The change was made by the constituent power of the Senate, and the senatus-consulte is dated May 18, 1804. The title of Emperor had an ulterior meaning. Adopted at the moment when Napoleon began to feel himself master both in Italy and Germany, it revived the memory of Charles the Great. To himself it was the more satisfactory on that account, and, strange to say, it gave satisfaction rather than offence to the Head of the Holy Roman Empire, Francis II. Since Joseph the Habsburg Emperors had been tired of their title, which, being elective, was precarious. They were desirous of becoming hereditary emperors in Austria, and they now took this title (though without as yet giving up the other). Francis II. bartered his acknowledgment of Napoleon's new title against Napoleon's acknowledgment of his own.

It required some impudence to condemn Moreau for royalism at the very moment that his rival was re-establishing monarchy. Yet his trial began on May 15th. The death of Pichegru, nominally by suicide, on April 6th had already furnished the rising sultanism with its first dark mystery. Moreau was condemned to two years' imprisonment, but was allowed to retire to the United States.

CHAPTER IV.

THE EMPEROR.

§ 1. *Designs against England and the Continent.— Napoleon crowned.*

THESE changes destroyed all that remained of the political life of France. Jacobinism had been eradicated in Nivose; republicanism and royalism were paralyzed now. Henceforth there was no power or person in France but Bonaparte; upon his absolute will a great nation and an unparalleled military force waited. He had undertaken to settle a dispute in which France had been engaged throughout the eighteenth century; he had undertaken to humble the might of England. Would not, then, ordinary prudence suggest to him the expediency of postponing any aggressive designs he might have on the continental Powers? He had done much since Brumaire to reconcile Europe to his government; it now became more obviously politic to tread the path of conciliation, while he assembled the forces of Europe under his leadership against the tyrant of the seas. Strange to say, he pursued the opposite course, and at the very time when his grand stroke against England was in suspense extended his power so recklessly in Italy, behaved with such insolence to the German Powers, and shocked public feeling by acts so Jacobinical, that he brought upon himself a new European coalition. It was the great mistake of his life. He was not, in the long run, a match for England and the continent together; he made at starting the irremediable mistake of not dividing these two enemies. He seems indeed to have set out with a monstrous miscalculation which might have ruined him very speedily, for he had laid his plan for an invasion of England and a war in Europe at the same time. If we imagine the invasion successfully begun, we see France thrown back into the position of 1799, her best general and army cut off from her by the sea, while Austria, Russia, and perhaps Prussia pour their armies across the Rhine; but we see that the position would have been far worse than in 1799, since France without Bonaparte in 1805 would have been wholly paralyzed. As it was, the signal failure of his English enterprise left room for a triumphant campaign in Germany, and

Ulm concealed Trafalgar from the view of the Continent.

The European Coalition had been disarmed since Brumaire by the belief that Bonaparte's Government was less intolerably aggressive than that of the Directory; this belief gave place in 1803 to a conviction that he was quite as aggressive and much more dangerous. England therefore might hope to revive the Coalition, and in the spring of 1804 she recalled Pitt to the helm in order that he might do this. The violent proceedings of Bonaparte on the occasion of the rupture, his occupation of Hanover, his persecution of the English representatives in Germany,—Spencer Smith at Stuttgart, Drake at Munich, Sir G. Rumbold at Hamburg,—created an alarm in the cabinets greater than that of 1798, and the murder of D'Enghien shocked as much as it alarmed them. Positive conquest and annexation of territory too now went on as rapidly and as openly as in 1798. The new empire compared itself to that of Charlemagne, which extended over Italy and Germany, and on December 2, 1804, a parody of the famous transference of the empire took place in Notre Dame, Pope Pius VII. appearing there to crown Napoleon, who however took the crown from his hands and placed it himself upon his own head.

Meanwhile the Italian republic was changed into a kingdom, which at first Bonaparte intended to give to his brother Joseph, but in the end accepted for himself. In the spring of 1805, fresh from the *sacre* in Notre Dame, he visited Italy and received the iron crown of the Lombard kings at Milan (May 26). A little later the Ligurian republic was annexed, and a principality was found for his brother-in-law Bacciochi in Lucca and Piombino. By these acts he seemed to show himself not only ready but eager to fight with all Europe at once. It was not his fault that in the autumn of 1805, when he fought with Austria and Russia in Germany, he was not also maintaining a desperate struggle in the heart of England; it was not his fault that Prussia was not also at war with him, for his aggressions had driven Prussia almost to despair, and only once — that is, in the matter of Sir G. Rumbold — had he shown the smallest consideration for her. And yet at first fortune did not seem to favor him.

Had public opinion been less enslaved in France, had the frivolity of the nation been less skilfully amused by the operatic exhibitions of the new court and the *sacre* in Notre Dame, it would have been remarked that, after most needlessly involving France in war with England, Bonaparte had suffered half the year 1803, all the year 1804, and again more than half the year 1805 to pass without striking a single blow, that after the most gigantic and costly preparations the scheme of invasion was given up, and that finally France suffered a crushing defeat at Trafalgar which paralyzed her on the side of England for the rest of the war. In order to understand in any degree the course he took, it seems necessary to suppose that the intoxication of the Marengo campaign still held him, that as then, contrary to all expectation, he had passed the Alps, crushed his enemy, and instantly returned, so now he made no doubt of passing the Channel, signing peace in London, and returning in a month with a fabulous indemnity in his pocket to meet the Coalition in Germany. To conquer England it was worth while to wait two years, but his position was very critical when, after losing two years, he was obliged to confess himself foiled. He retrieved his position suddenly, and achieved a triumph which, though less complete than that which he had counted on, was still prodigious, — the greatest triumph of his life. At the moment when his English scheme was ending in deplorable failure, he produced another, less gigantic but more solid, which he unfolded with a rapid precision and secrecy peculiar to himself. In the five years which had passed since Marengo his position for the purposes of a Continental war had improved vastly. Then he had no footing either in Germany or Italy, and his new office of First Consul gave him a very precarious control over the armies, which themselves were in a poor condition. Now his military authority was absolute, and the armies after five years of imperialism were in perfect organization; he had North Italy to the Adige; and since the Germanic revolution of 1803 Bavaria, Würtemberg, and Baden had passed over to his side. Therefore, as the Coalition consisted only of Austria, Russia, and England, he might count upon success, and the more confidently if he could strike Austria before the arrival of the Russian army. It is strange that in this estimate it should be unnecessary to take Prussia into the account, since the Prussian army (consisting of 250,000 men) was at that time supposed to be a match by itself for the French. But for ten years Prussia had striven to hold a middle course, almost equally distrustful of France on the one side and of her old rival Austria, or her powerful neighbor Russia, on the other. She still clung convulsively to her strange system of immovable neutrality, and in this war both sides had to put up with the uncertainty whether the prodigious weight of the army of Frederick would not be thrown suddenly either into its own or into the opposite scale. It was at the end of August, 1805, that Napoleon made his sudden change of front. At the beginning of that month he had been still intent on the invasion of England; ever since March maritime manœuvres on an unparalleled scale had been carried on with the object of decoying the English fleets away from the Channel, and so giving an opportunity for the army of invasion to cross it on a flotilla under the protection of French fleets. But in spite of all manœuvres a great English fleet remained stationary at Brest, and Nelson, having been for a moment decoyed to Barbados, returned again. In the last days of August Admiral Villeneuve, issuing from Ferrol, took alarm at the news of the approach of an English fleet, and instead of sailing northward faced about and retired to Cadiz. Then for the first time Napoleon admitted the idea of failure, and saw the necessity of screening it by some great achievement in another quarter. He resolved to throw his whole force upon the Coalition, and to do it suddenly. Prussia was to be bribed by the very substantial present of Hanover.

§ 2. *Campaign against Austria and Russia.— Capitulation of Ulm.— Battle of Austerlitz.— War with Prussia.— Treaty of Tilsit.*

Five years had passed since Napoleon had taken the field when the second period of his military career began. He now begins to make war as a sovereign with a boundless command of means. For five years from 1805 to 1809 he takes the field regularly, and in these campaigns he founds the great Napoleonic empire. By the first he breaks up the Germanic system and attaches the minor German states to France, by the second he humbles Prussia, by the third he forces Russia into an alliance, by the fourth he reduces Spain to submission, by the fifth he humbles Austria. Then follows a second pause during which for three years Napoleon's sword is in the sheath, and he is once more ruler, not soldier.

It is to be observed that he sets out with no distinct design of conquest, but only because he has been attacked by the Coalition. Fortune then tempts him on from triumph to triumph, and throughout he has no other conscious design but to turn all the force of the Continent against England.

Napoleon's strategy always aims at an overwhelming surprise. As in 1800, when all eyes were intent on Genoa, and from Genoa the Austrians hoped to penetrate into France, he created an overwhelming confusion by throwing himself across the Alps and marching not upon Genoa but upon Milan, so now he appeared not in front of the Austrians but behind them and between them and Vienna. The wavering faith of Bavaria had caused the Austrians to pass the Inn and to advance across the country to Ulm. It was intended that the Russians should join them here, and that the united host should invade France, taking Napoleon, as they fondly hoped, by surprise. It is to be remarked that of all the coalitions this seems to have been the most loosely combined, owing chiefly to the shallowness and inexperience of Alexander. Austria was hurried into action, and found herself unsupported at need by the Russians, and disappointed altogether of the help of Prussia, upon which she had counted. Moreover, so often unfortunate in her choice of generals, she had this time made the most unfortunate choice of all. Mack, who at Naples in 1799 had moved the impatient contempt of Nelson, now stood matched against Napoleon at the height of his power. He occupied the line of the Iller from Ulm to Memmingen, expecting the attack of Napoleon, who personally lingered at Strasburg, in front. Meanwhile the

French armies swarmed from Hanover and down the Rhine, treating the small German states half as allies half as conquered dependants, and disregarding all neutrality, even that of Prussia, till they took up their positions along the Danube from Donauwörth to Ratisbon far in the rear of Mack. The surprise was so complete that Mack, who in the early days of October used the language of confident hope, on the 17th surrendered at Ulm with about 26,000 men, while another division, that of Werneck, surrendered on the 18th to Murat at Nördlingen. In a month the whole Austrian army, consisting of 80,000 men, was entirely dissolved. Napoleon was master of Bavaria, recalled the elector to Munich, and received the congratulations of the electors of Würtemberg and Baden (they had just at this time the title of electors). It was the stroke of Marengo repeated, but without a doubtful battle and without undeserved good luck.

After Marengo it had been left to Moreau to win the decisive victory and to conclude the war; this time there was no Moreau to divide the laurels. The second part of the campaign begins at once; on October 28 Napoleon reports that a division of his army has crossed the Inn. He has now to deal with the Russians, of whom 40,000 men have arrived under Kutusoff. He reaches Linz on November 4, where Gyulai brought him the emperor's proposals for an armistice. He replies by demanding Venice and Tyrol, and insisting upon the exclusion of Russia from the negotiations, conditions which, as he no doubt foresaw, Gyulai did not think himself authorized to accept. But Napoleon did not intend this time, as in 1797 and in 1800, to stop short of Vienna. Nothing now could resist his advance, for the other Austrian armies, that of the archduke John in Tyrol and that of the archduke Charles on the Adige, were held in play by Ney and Masséna, and compelled at last, instead of advancing to the rescue, to retire through Carniola into Hungary. On November 14 he dates from the palace of Schönbrunn; on the day before Murat had entered Vienna, which the Austrian emperor, from motives of humanity, had resolved not to defend, and the French also succeeded by an unscrupulous trick in getting possession of the bridges over the Danube. So far his progress had been triumphant, and yet he was now in an extremely critical position. The archduke Charles was approaching from Hungary with 80,000 Austrians; another Russian army was entering Moravia to join Kutusoff, who had with great skill escaped from the pursuit of Murat after the capture of Vienna. Napoleon, though he had brought 200,000 men into Germany, had not now, since he was obliged to keep open his communications down the valley of the Danube, a large army available for the field. But, what was much more serious, he had recklessly driven Prussia into the opposite camp. He had marched troops across her territory of Ansbach, violating her neutrality, and in consequence on November 3 (while Napoleon was at Linz) she had signed with Russia the treaty of Potsdam, which practically placed 180,000 of the most highly drilled troops in the world at the service of the Coalition. Such had been Napoleon's rashness, for his audacious daring was balanced indeed by infinite cunning and ingenuity, but was seldom tempered by prudence. In this position, it may be asked, how could he expect ever to make his way back to France? What he had done to Mack Prussia would now do to him. The army of Frederick would block the Danube between him and France, while the Russians and Austrians, united under the archduke, would seek him at Vienna.

As at Marengo, fortune favored his hazardous strategy. The allies had only to play a waiting game, but this the Russians and their young Czar, who was now in the Moravian head-quarters, would not consent to do. He was surrounded by young and rash counsellors, and the Russians, remembering the victories of Suwaroff in 1799, and remarking that almost all Napoleon's victories hitherto had been won over Austrians, had not yet learned to be afraid of him. Napoleon became aware of their sanguine confidence from Savary, whom he had sent to the Czar with proposals; he contrived to heighten it by exhibiting his army as ill-prepared to Dolgorouki, sent to him on the part of the Czar. The end was that the Russians (80,000 men, aided by about 15,000 Austrians) rushed into the battle of Austerlitz (December 2, 1805), which brought the third Coalition to an end, as that of Hohenlinden had brought the second. Nowhere was Napoleon's superiority more manifest; the Russians lost more than 20,000 men, the Austrians 6,000. The former retired at once under a military convention, and before the year 1805 was out the treaty at Pressburg was concluded with Austria (December 26) and that of Schönbrunn with Prussia (December 15).

It was a transformation scene more bewildering than even that of Marengo, and completely altered the position of Napoleon before Europe. To the French indeed Austerlitz was not, as a matter of exultation, equal to Marengo, for it did not deliver the state from danger, but only raised it from a perilous eminence to an eminence more perilous still. But as a military achievement it was far greater, exhibiting the army at the height of its valor and organization (the illusion of liberty not yet quite dissipated), and the commander at the height of his tactical skill; and in its historical results it is greater still, ranking among the great events of the world. For not only did it found the ephemeral Napoleonic empire by handing over Venetia to the Napoleonic monarchy of Italy, and Tyrol and Vorarlberg to Napoleon's new client Bavaria; it also destroyed the Holy Roman Empire, while it divided the remains of Hither Austria between Würtemberg and Baden. In the summer of 1806 the emperor of Austria (he had this title since 1804) solemnly abdicated the title of Roman emperor; the ancient diet of Ratisbon was dissolved, and a new organization was created under the name of Confederation of the Rhine, in which the minor states of Germany were united under the protectorate of Napoleon, much in the same way as in former times they had been united under the presidency of Austria. Bavaria and Würtemberg at the same time were raised into kingdoms. In all the changes which have happened since, the Holy Roman Empire has never been revived, and this event remains the greatest in the modern history of Germany.

But Austerlitz was greater than Marengo in another way. That victory had a tranquillizing effect, and was soon followed by a peace which lasted more than four years. But the equilibrium established after Austerlitz was of the most unstable kind; it was but momentary, and was followed by a succession of the most appalling convulsions; the very report of the battle hastened the death of William Pitt. A French ascendency had existed since 1797, and Napoleon's Government had at first promised to make it less intolerable. Since 1803 this hope had vanished, but now suddenly the ascendency was converted into something like a universal monarchy. Europe could not settle down. The first half of 1806 was devoted to the internal reconstruction of Germany, and to the negotiation of peace with the two great belligerents who remained after Austria and Prussia had retired, viz., England and Russia. But these negotiations failed, and in failing revived the Coalition. On the side of England, Fox showed unexpectedly all the firmness of Pitt; and the Czar refused his ratification to the treaty which his representative at Paris, D'Oubril, had signed. Everything now depended on Prussia, and again Napoleon adopted the strange policy by which a year before he had armed all Europe against himself. Instead of detaching Prussia from the Coalition by friendly advances, he drives her into it by his reckless insolence. At a moment when she found herself almost shut out of the German world by the new Confederation, Napoleon was found coolly treating with England for the restoration of Hanover to George III. In August, 1806, just at the moment of the dissolution of the Holy Roman Empire and the formation of the Confederation of the Rhine, Prussia suddenly mobilized her army, and about the same time Russia rejected the treaty. This amounted practically to a new Coalition, or to a revival of the old one with Prussia in the place of Austria. On September 10 he writes, 'The Prussians wish to receive a lesson.' No one knew so well as Napoleon the advantage given by suddenness and rapidity. The year before he had succeeded in crushing the Austrians before the Russians could come up; against Prussia he had now the advantage that she had long been politically isolated, and could not immediately get help either from Russia or England,— for the moment only Saxony and Hessen-Cassel stood by her,— while his armies, to the number of 200,000 men, were already stationed in Bavaria and Swabia, whence in a few days they could arrive on the scene of action. The year before Austria had been ruined by the incapacity of Mack; Prussia now suffered from an incapacity diffused through the higher ranks both of the military and civil service. Generals too old, such as Brunswick and Möllendorf, a military system corrupted by long peace, a policy without clearness, a diplomacy without honor, had converted the great power founded by Frederick into a body without a soul. There began a new war, of which the incidents are almost precisely parallel to those of the war which had so lately closed. As the Austrians at Ulm, so now Napoleon crushed the Prussians at Jena and Auerstädt (October 14) before the appearance of the Russians; as he entered Vienna, so now he enters Berlin (October 27); as he fought a second war in Moravia, in which Austria played a second part to Russia, so now from November, 1806, to June, 1807, he fights in East Prussia against the Russians aided with smaller numbers by the Prussians; as he might then, after all his successes, have been ruined by the intervention of Prussia, so now, had Austria struck in, he might have found much difficulty in making his way back to France; as at Austerlitz, so at Friedland in June, 1807, the Russians ran hastily into a decisive battle, in which they ruined their ally but not themselves; as Austria at Pressburg, so Prussia at Tilsit signed a most humiliating treaty, while Russia, as before, escaped, not this time by simply retiring from the scene, but by a treaty in which Napoleon admitted her to a share in the spoils of victory.

Here was a second catastrophe far more surprising and disastrous than that which it followed so closely. The defeat of Austria in 1805 had been similar to her former defeats in 1800 and 1797; Ulm had been similar to Hohenlinden, the treaty of Pressburg to that of Lunéville. But the double repulse of Jena and Auerstädt, which threw two armies back upon each other, and so ruined both, dissolved forever the military creation of the great Frederick; and it was followed by a general panic, surrender of fortresses, and submission on the part of civil officials, which seemed almost to amount to a dissolution of the Prussian state. The defence of Colberg by Gneisenau and the conduct of the Prussian troops under Lestocq at Eylau, were almost the only redeeming achievements of the famous army which, half a century before, had withstood for seven years the attack of three

Great Powers at once. This downfall was expressed in the treaty of Tilsit, which was vastly more disastrous to Prussia than that of Pressburg had been to Austria. Prussia was partitioned between Saxony, Russia, and a newly established Napoleonic kingdom of Westphalia. Her population was reduced by one-half, her army from 250,000 to 42,000 (the number fixed a little later by the treaty of September, 1808), and Napoleon contrived also by a trick to saddle her for some time with the support of a French army of 150,000 men. She was in fact, and continued till 1813 to be, a conquered state. Russia, on the other hand, came off with more credit, as well as with less loss, than in the former campaign. At Eylau in January, 1807, she in part atoned for Austerlitz. It was, perhaps, the most murderous battle that had been fought since the wars began, and it was not a defeat. Friedland, too, was well contested.

Another great triumph for Napoleon! But he might reflect at a later time that he had converted Prussia, which for ten years had been the most friendly to France of all the great Powers, into her most embittered enemy. On April 26, by the treaty of Bartenstein, Prussia had joined in all form the European Coalition.

§ 3. *Napoleon as King of Kings.*

In the two years between August, 1805, and the treaty of Tilsit Napoleon had drifted far from his first plan of an invasion of England. But he seemed brought back to it now by another route. England had marshalled Europe against him; might he not now marshal Europe against England? Austria was humbled, Prussia beneath his feet. Why should Russia for the future side with England against him? From the outset her interest in the wars of the West had been but slight; under Catherine it had been hypocritically feigned, in order to divert the eyes of Europe from her Eastern conquests; and perhaps Alexander, in 1805 and 1806, had not been free from a similar hypocrisy. The Russians themselves felt this so much that after Friedland they forced Alexander to abandon the new combination so recently arranged at Bartenstein, and to make peace. But as Paul, when he left the Second Coalition, had actually joined France, Napoleon now saw the means of making Alexander do the same. England's tyranny of the seas had been attacked by the great Catherine and again by Paul; on this subject, therefore, Russian policy might co-operate with Napoleon, and, if its real object was only to obtain freedom in Turkey, this could be gained as well by a direct understanding with Napoleon as by giving occupation to his arms in Germany. Such was the basis of the treaty of Tilsit, negotiated between Napoleon and Alexander on an island in the river Niemen, with which treaty commences a new phase in the struggle between Napoleon and England. Russia not only abandons England, but combines with France to humble her. Hitherto we have heard of coalitions against France, of which England has been the soul or at least the paymaster. At Tilsit Napoleon founds a European coalition against England.

A pause occurs after Friedland, during which Europe begins slowly to realize her position, and to penetrate the character of Napoleon. It took some time to wear out his reputation of peacemaker; at his breach with England in 1803 he had appealed to that jealousy of England's maritime power which was widely spread; many thought the war was forced upon him, and as to the war of 1805, it could not be denied that Austria and Russia had attacked him. His absolute control over the French press enabled him almost to dictate public opinion.

But the conquest of Germany, achieved in little more time than had sufficed to Bonaparte ten years before for the conquest of Italy, put him in a new light. He had already passed through many phases: he had been the invincible champion of liberty, then the destroyer of Jacobinism and champion of order, then the new Constantine and restorer of the church, then the pacificator of the world, then the founder of a new monarchy in France. Now suddenly, in 1807, he stands forth in the new character of head of a great European confederacy. It has been usual to contrast the consulate with the empire, but the great transformation was made by the wars of 1805-7, and the true contrast is between the man of Brumaire and the man of Tilsit. The empire as founded in 1804 did not perhaps differ so much from the consulate after Marengo as both differed, alike in spirit and form, from the empire such as it began to appear after Pressburg and was consolidated after Tilsit. Between 1800 and 1805 Napoleon, under whatever title, was absolute ruler of France, including Belgium, the left bank of the Rhine, Savoy and Nice, and practically also ruler of Holland, Switzerland, and North Italy to the Adige, which states had a republican form. The title emperor meant in 1804 little more than military ruler. But now emperor has rather its mediæval meaning of paramount over a confederacy of princes. Napoleon has become a king of kings. This system had been commenced in the consulate, when a kingdom of Etruria under the consul's protection was created for the benefit of his ally, the King of Spain; it was carried a stage further on the eve of the war of 1805, when the kingdom of Italy was created, of which Napoleon himself assumed the sceptre, but committed the government to Eugène Beauharnais as viceroy. But now almost all Italy and a great part of Germany is subjected to this system. The Bonaparte family, which before had contended for the succession in France, so that Joseph actually refuses, as beneath him, the crown of Italy, now accept subordinate crowns. Joseph becomes King of Naples, the Bourbon dynasty having been expelled immediately after the peace of Pressburg; Louis becomes King of Holland; Jerome, the youngest brother, receives after Tilsit a kingdom of Westphalia, composed of territory taken from Prussia, of Hanover, and of the electorate of Hessen-Cassel, which had shared the fall of Prussia; somewhat earlier Murat, husband of the most ambitious of the Bonaparte sisters, Caroline, had received the grand-duchy of Berg. By the side of these Bonaparte princes there are the German princes who now look up to France, as under the Holy Roman Empire they had looked up to Austria. These are formed into a Confederation in which the Archbishop of Mainz (Dalberg) presides, as he had before presided in the empire. Two of the princes have now the title of kings, and, enriched as they are by the secularization of church lands, the mediatization of immediate nobles, and the subjugation of free cities, they have also the substantial power. A princess of Bavaria weds Eugène Beauharnais, a princess of Würtemberg Jerome Bonaparte. At its foundation in 1806 the Confederation had twelve members, but in the end it came to include almost all the states of Germany except Austria and Prussia.

A change seems to take place at the same time in Napoleon's personal relations. In 1804, though the divorce of Josephine was debated, yet it appears to be Napoleon's fixed intention to bequeath his crown by the method of adoption to the eldest son of Louis by Hortense Beauharnais. But this child died suddenly of croup on May 5, 1807, while Napoleon was absent in Germany, and the event, occurring at the moment when he attained his position of king of kings, probably decided him in his own mind to proceed to the divorce.

It was impossible to give crowns and principalities to the Bonaparte family without allowing a share of similar distinctions to the leading politicians and generals of France. He was therefore driven to revive titles of nobility. To do this was to abandon the revolutionary principle of equality, but Napoleon always bore in mind the necessity of bribing in the most splendid manner the party upon whose support ever since Brumaire he had depended, and which may be described shortly as the Senate. When in 1802 he received the life-consulate, he had proceeded instantly to create new dotations for the senators; now he feels that he must devise for them still more splendid bribes. His first plan is to give them feudal lordships outside France. Thus Berthier, his most indispensable minister, becomes sovereign prince of Neufchatel, Bernadotte sovereign prince of Pontecorvo, Talleyrand sovereign prince of Benevento. Especially out of the Venetian territory, given to France at Pressburg, are taken fiefs (not less than twelve in all), to which are attached the title of duke. These innovations fall in 1806, that is, in the middle of the period of transformation. But after Tilsit, when Napoleon felt more strongly both the power and the necessity of rewarding his servants, he created formally a new noblesse, and revived the *majorat* in defiance of the revolutionary code. In the end, besides the three sovereign princes just mentioned, he created four hereditary princes (Berthier is in both lists) and thirty-one hereditary dukes. There were also many counts and barons. The system was prodigiously wasteful. Of public money Berthier received more than £50,000 a year, Davoust about £30,000, nine other officials more than £10,000, and twenty-three others more than £4,000.

After Marengo he had seen the importance of reconciling Europe to his greatness by making peace. After Tilsit it was still more urgently necessary that he should dispel the alarm which his conquests had now excited everywhere. But this time he made no attempt to do so; this time he can think of nothing but pushing his success to the destruction of England; and Europe gradually became aware that the evil so long dreaded of a destruction of the balance of power had come in the very worst form conceivable, and that her destiny was in the hands of a man whose headlong ambition was as unprecedented as his energy and good fortune.

As in 1805 he had been drawn into the conquest of Germany in the course of a war with England, so now he assails all the neutral powers, and shortly afterwards violently annexes Spain, not so much from abstract love of conquest as in order to turn against England the forces of all the Continent at once. As he had left Boulogne for Germany, he now, as it were, returns to Boulogne. His successes had put into his hands two new instruments of war against England, instruments none the less welcome because the very act of using them made him master of the whole Continent. He had hinted at the first of these when the war with England began in 1803, by saying that in this war he did not intend that there should be any neutrality. What he meant was explained in 1806 by the edict issued from Berlin. In addition to that limited right, which the belligerent has by international law, to prevent by blockade the trade of a neutral with the enemy and to punish the individual trader by confiscation of ship and goods, Napoleon now assumed the right of preventing such commerce without blockade by controlling the neutral governments. English goods were to be seized everywhere, and the harbors of neutrals to be closed against English ships under penalty of war with France. Such a threat, involving a claim to criticise and judge the acts of neutral governments, and to inflict on them an enormous pecuniary fine, was almost equivalent to the annexation at one stroke of all the neutral states. The other instrument had a similar character. The French fleet having been crippled at Trafalgar, he proposed now to reinforce it by all the other fleets in Europe, and to get possession of all the resources of all the maritime states. His eyes therefore become now fixed on Denmark, Portugal, and Spain.

Such is Napoleon as king of kings, and such are his views. This unique phase of European history lasted five years, reckoning from the treaty of Tilsit to the breach with Russia. Europe consists now of a confederacy of monarchical states looking up to a paramount power (like India at the present day). The confederacy is held together by the war with England, which it puts under an ineffective commercial blockade, suffering itself in return a more effective one. But Napoleon feels that Spain and Portugal must be brought under his immediate administration, in order that their maritime resources may be properly turned against England.

It cannot be necessary to point out that this method of attacking England was essentially ill-judged, however marvellous the display of power to which it gave rise. The confederacy was held together by the weakest of bonds, viz. by sheer force. What was unsatisfactorily achieved by the miracles of Austerlitz, Jena, and Friedland, might have been accomplished far better without them by diplomacy acting on the wide-spread jealousy and dislike of England. Napoleon's confederacy might always be suspected of wishing to pass over to the side of England, as at last it did. Austria begins to meditate a new war on the morrow of Pressburg, and Prussia is humbled so intolerably that she is forced into plans of insurrection. Throughout these five years a European party of insurrection is gradually forming. It has two great divisions, one scattered through Germany, at the head of which Austria places herself in 1809, the other in Spain and Portugal, which is aided by England. In Germany this movement is successfully repressed until 1813, but in the Peninsula it gains ground steadily from 1809. After 1812 both movements swell the great Anti-Napoleonic Revolution which then sets in.

CHAPTER V.

REBELLION.

§ 1. *French Army in Spain. — Popular Rising in Spain. — Napoleon in Spain.*

IMMEDIATELY after Tilsit Napoleon entered on his new course, which had been arranged with Russia in secret articles. In August he required the King of Denmark to declare war with England; but here England, seeing herself threatened by a coalition of all Europe at once, interfered with desperate resolution. She required Denmark to surrender her fleet (consisting of twenty ships of the line and a number of frigates) in deposit, promising to restore it at the peace; on receiving a refusal she took possession of it by force. At the same time he formed an army under Junot for the invasion of Portugal, with which state, as the old ally of England, Napoleon used no ceremony. The feeble government consented to almost all his demands, agreed to enter the Continental system and to declare war against

England; only the regent had a scruple which restrained him from confiscating the property of private Englishmen. From this moment Portugal is doomed, and negotiations are opened with Spain concerning the partition of it. But out of these negotiations grew unexpected events.

For more than ten years Spain had been drawn in the wake of revolutionary France. To Napoleon from the beginning of his reign she had been as subservient as Holland or Switzerland; she had made war and peace at his bidding, had surrendered Trinidad to make the treaty of Amiens, had given her fleet to destruction at Trafalgar. In other states equally subservient, such as Holland and the Italian Republic, Napoleon had remodelled the government at his pleasure, and in the end had put his own family at the head of it. After Tilsit he thought himself strong enough to make a similar change in Spain, and the occupation of Portugal seemed to afford the opportunity of doing this. By two conventions signed at Fontainebleau on October 27 the partition of Portugal was arranged with Spain. The Prince of the Peace was to become a sovereign prince of the Algarves, the King of Spain was to have Brazil with the title of Emperor of the two Americas, &c.; but the main provision was that a French army was to stand on the threshold of Spain ready to resist any intervention of England. The occupation of Portugal took place soon after, Junot arriving at Lisbon on November 30, just as the royal family with a following of several thousands set sail for Brazil under protection of the English fleet. At the same time there commenced in defiance of all treaties a passage of French troops into Spain, which continued until 80,000 had arrived, and had taken quiet possession of a number of Spanish fortresses. At last Murat was appointed to the command of the army of Spain. He entered the country on March 1, 1808, and marched on Madrid, calculating that the king would retire and take refuge at Seville or Cadiz. This act revealed to the world, and even to a large party among the French themselves, the nature of the power which had been created at Tilsit. The lawless acts of Napoleon's earlier life were palliated by the name of the French Revolution, and since Brumaire he had established a character for comparative moderation. But here was naked violence without the excuse of fanaticism; and on what a scale! One of the greater states of Europe was in the hands of a burglar, who would moreover, if successful, become king not only of Spain but of a boundless empire in the New World.

The sequel was worse even than this commencement, although the course which events took seems to show that by means of a little delay he might have attained his end without such open defiance of law. The administration of Spain had long been in the contemptible hands of Manuel Godoy, supposed to be the queen's lover, yet at the same time high in the favor of King Charles IV. Ferdinand, the heir apparent, headed an opposition, but in character he was not better than the trio he opposed, and he had lately been put under arrest on suspicion of designs upon his father's life. To have fomented this opposition without taking either side, and to have rendered both sides equally contemptible to the Spanish people, was Napoleon's game. The Spanish people, who profoundly admired him, might then have been induced to ask him for a king. Napoleon, however, perpetrated his crime before the scandal of the palace broke out. The march of Murat now brought it to a head. On March 17 a tumult broke out at Aranjuez, which led to the fall of the favorite, and then to the abdication of the king, and the proclamation of Ferdinand amid universal truly Spanish enthusiasm. It was a fatal mistake to have forced on this popular explosion, and Napoleon has characteristically tried to conceal it by a supposititious letter, dated March 29, in which he tries to throw the blame upon Murat, to whom the letter professes to be addressed. It warns Murat against rousing Spanish patriotism and creating an opposition of the nobles and clergy, which will lead to a *levée en masse*, and to a war without end. It predicts, in short, all that took place, but it has every mark of invention, and was certainly never received by Murat. The reign of Ferdinand having thus begun, all that the French could do was to abstain from acknowledging him, and to encourage Charles to withdraw his abdication as given under duress. By this means it became doubtful who was king of Spain, and Napoleon, having carefully refrained from taking a side, now presented himself as arbiter. Ferdinand was induced to betake himself to Napoleon's presence at Bayonne, where he arrived on April 21; his father and mother followed on the 30th. Violent scenes took place between father and son: news arrived of an insurrection at Madrid and of the stern suppression of it by Murat. In the end Napoleon succeeded in extorting the abdication both of Charles and Ferdinand. It was learned too late that the insurrection of Spain had not really been suppressed.

This crime, as clumsy as it was monstrous, brought on that great popular insurrection of

Europe against the universal monarchy, which has profoundly modified all subsequent history, and makes the Anti-Napoleonic Revolution an event of the same order as the French Revolution. A rising unparalleled for its suddenness and sublime spontaneousness took place throughout Spain and speedily found a response in Germany. A new impulse was given, out of which grew the great nationality movement of the nineteenth century. Meanwhile Napoleon, having first offered the throne of Spain to his brother Louis, who refused it, named Joseph king, retaining, however, a reversion to himself and heirs in default of male heirs of Joseph, who had only daughters. The royal council first, afterwards a junta of nobles assembled at Bayonne, accepted him on July 7. But it must have become clear to Napoleon almost at once that he had committed the most enormous of blunders. Instead of gaining Spain he had in fact lost it, for hitherto he had been master of its resources without trouble, whereas to support Joseph he was obliged in this same year to invade Spain in person with not less than 180,000 men. With Spain too he lost Portugal, which in June followed the Spanish example of insurrection, and had Spain henceforth for an ally and not for an enemy. Hitherto he had had no serious conception of any kind of war not strictly professional. He had known popular risings in Italy, La Vendée, and Egypt, but had never found it at all difficult to crush them. The determined insurrection of a whole nation of 11,000,000 was a new experience to him. How serious it might be he learned as early as July, when Dupont, with about 20,000 men, surrendered at Baylen in Andalusia to the Spanish General Castaños. In August he might wake to another miscalculation of which he had been guilty. An English army landed in Portugal, defeated Junot at Vimeiro, and forced him to sign the convention of Cintra. By this he evacuated Portugal, in which country the insurrection had already left him much isolated. This occurrence brought to light a capital feature of the insurrection of the Peninsula, viz. that it was in free communication everywhere with the power and resources of England.

The Spanish affair is the best illustration of the insensate blindness which marks the imperial period of Napoleon. It shows him wedded to a system of violence which yields little gain when it is most successful, and causes prodigious loss when it is in any degree unsuccessful. On the whole, in 1808 he is not stronger than in 1803, but far weaker; for in 1803 he had in Italy, Germany, and Spain a prodigious ascendency, which did not require to be supported everywhere by armies, and did not yet excite hatred, but was regarded in Spain with enthusiasm, in Prussia with friendly equanimity, even in Austria with resignation. All he has done since is to convert this ascendency into actual government, but in the conversion more than half of it has escaped. Austria and Prussia are preparing for resistance to the death; Spain has begun it already, and has passed over to the English from the French coalition.

Thus the monarchy of Tilsit suffered within a year the most terrible rebuff. Napoleon himself now appears upon the scene. His first step was to revive the memory of Tilsit by a theatrical meeting with Alexander, which was arranged at Erfurt in September. The power of the duumvirate was there displayed in the most imposing manner, and the alliance was strengthened by new engagements taken by Napoleon with respect to the Danubian principalities. At the same time he checked the rising spirit of resistance in Prussia by driving from office the great reforming minister Stein. At the beginning of November he was ready for the invasion of Spain. Joseph had retired to Vittoria, and the armies of the insurrection fronted him along the Ebro under the command of Blake, Castaños, and Palafox. Between November 7 and 11 the army of Blake was dissolved by Lefebvre, and Napoleon entered Burgos, which was mercilessly pillaged; on the 23d Castaños was defeated at Tudela by Lannes; by December 2 Napoleon, having forced the mountain passes, was before Madrid, and on the 4th he was in possession of the town, where, endeavoring somewhat late to conciliate the liberalism of Europe, he proclaimed the abolition of the Inquisition and of feudalism, and the reduction of the number of convents to one-third. He remained in Spain till the middle of January, 1809, but he was not allowed repose during the interval. Sir John Moore had advanced from Portugal as far as Salamanca, and determined in the middle of December to assist the insurrection by marching on Valladolid. Soult was at Carrion and was threatened by this advance, since the English force, after Moore had effected his junction with Baird, who arrived from Corunna, at Majorga, amounted to 25,000 men. Napoleon hoped to cut its communications, and so deal one of his crushing blows at the enemy with whom he was always at war, yet whom he never, except at

Waterloo, met in the field. He set out on the 22d with about 40,000 men, and marched 200 miles in ten days over mountains in the middle of winter. Moore saw the danger, retired to Benavente, and blew up the bridges over the Ezla. Napoleon advanced as far as Astorga (Jan. 1); but he had missed his mark, and professed to receive information which showed him that he was urgently wanted at Paris. He returned to Valladolid, whence on January 17 he set out for France. The end of Moore's expedition belongs to English history.

§ 2. *First German War of Liberation.— Battle of Wagram. — Treaty of Schönbrunn. — War with Russia impending. — Divorce of Josephine. — Marriage with Marie Louise.*

Another storm was indeed gathering. Austria had been reduced to despair by the blows she had received, first at Pressburg, then at Tilsit, and the fate of the royal house of Spain seemed like a warning to that of Austria. But the year that followed Tilsit offered her a chance, which she grasped as a last chance. Spain, which formerly had given Napoleon help, now swallowed up 300,000 of his troops, so that in the autumn of 1808 he had been obliged to withdraw from Prussia the large army which he had kept for more than a year quartered on that unhappy country. Napoleon could spare henceforth only half his force, and there was now no doubt that Prussia would be as hostile to him as she dared. True, the army of Frederick had ceased to exist, but the country was full of soldiers who had belonged to it, full of skilled officers, and Spain had filled all minds with the thought of popular war. Stein and Scharnhorst had been preparing a *levée en masse* in Prussia and an insurrection in the new kingdom of Westphalia. Moreover the Austrian statesmen thought they saw an opposition to Napoleon rising at home under the leadership of Talleyrand, and they thought also that the Spanish affair had alienated Alexander. It was reported that Talleyrand had said to Alexander at Erfurt, 'Sire, you are civilized and your nation is not; we are civilized and our Sovereign is not; you therefore are our natural ally.' Such considerations and illusions caused the war of 1809, which may be called the First German War of Liberation, under the leadership of Austria. It was welcomed by Napoleon, who wanted new victories to retrieve his position. His superiority, though on the wane, was still enormous. Through the Confederation of the Rhine he had now a great German army at his disposal, which he placed under French generals. His frontier was most formidably advanced through the possession of Tyrol and Venetia. Russia was on his side, and, though she did not actively help him in the field, was of great use in holding down Prussia; England was against him, but could do little for an inland state such as Austria now was. In these circumstances the attitude of Austria had something heroic about it, like that of Spain, and the war throughout is like a somewhat pale copy of the Spanish insurrection. But Austria has what Spain had not, the advantage of organization and intelligence. Since Pressburg she had passed through a period of reform and shown some signs of moral regeneration, Stadion and the archduke Charles doing for her, though not so effectively, what Stein and Scharnhorst did for Prussia. Few wars have begun with less ostensible ground, or more evidently from an intolerable position. Napoleon accused Austria of arming, of wanting war; Austria expostulated, but in vain; and war began. It began early in April, and the proclamation of the archduke Charles was addressed to the whole German nation. The watchword of Austria against France was now liberty and nationality. A good general conception of the war may be obtained by comparing it with that of 1805, which it resembles in certain large features. Again there is a short but decisive passage of arms in Bavaria; in a five days' struggle, celebrated for Napoleon's masterly manœuvres, the Austrians are driven out of Ratisbon (April 23), and the way to Vienna is laid open. Again Napoleon enters Vienna (May 13). But the war in Italy this time begins farther east, on the Piave. Eugène Beauharnais, after an unfortunate commencement, when he was defeated at Sacile by the archduke John, makes a successful advance, and being joined by Marmont, who makes his way to him from Dalmatia by way of Fiume, drives the Austrian army into Hungary, defeats them at Raab, and effects a junction with Napoleon at Bruck. Then, as before, the war is transferred from Vienna to the other side of the Danube. But the Austrian resistance is now far more obstinate than in 1805. From the island of Lobau Napoleon throws his troops across the river in the face of the archduke. A battle takes place which occupies two successive days (May 21, 22), and is sometimes called the battle of the Marchfeld, but is sometimes named from the villages of Gross-Aspern and Essling. It stands with that of Eylau in 1807 among the most terrible and bloody battles of the period. In all perhaps 50,000 men fell, among whom was Marshal Lannes, and the French were driven back into their island. Five weeks passed in inaction before Napoleon could retrieve this check, five weeks during which the condition of Europe was indeed singular, since its whole destiny depended upon a single man, and he, besides the ordinary risks of a campaign, was threatened by an able adversary who had recently brought him to the verge of destruction, and by outraged populations which might rise in insurrection round him. This is the moment of the glory of Hofer, the hero of the peasant war in Tyrol. Once more, however, Napoleon's skill and fortune prevailed. On the night of July 4th he succeeded, under cover of a false attack, in throwing six bridges from Lobau to the left bank of the Danube, over which more than 100,000 men passed before morning, and were arrayed upon the Marchfeld. The obstinate battle of Wagram followed, in which, by a miscalculation which became the subject of much controversy, the archduke John came too late to his brother's help. The Austrians were worsted, but by no means decisively, and retired in good order.

Austerlitz and Friedland had led at once to peace, because the principal belligerent, Russia, had little direct interest in the war; Wagram ought to have had no similar effect. Austria was engaged in a war of liberation; Tyrol was emulating Spain; there should therefore have been no negotiation with the invader. But Germany had as yet but half learnt the Spanish principle of war; in particular the Austrian Government and the archduke Charles himself belonged to Old Austria rather than to New Germany. In the campaign the archduke had fallen much below his reputation, having allowed it plainly to appear that Napoleon frightened him, and now, instead of appealing again to German patriotism, he signed at Znaim (July 11th) an armistice similar to that which Melas had so unaccountably concluded after Marengo. But it was by no means certain that all was yet over. North Germany might rise, as Spain had risen and as Tyrol had risen. The archduke Ferdinand had marched into Poland and threatened Thorn, with the intention of provoking such a movement in Prussia, and England was preparing a great armament which the patriots of North Germany, who now began to emulate the Spanish guerilla leaders, — Schill, Dörnberg, Katt, Brunswick, — anxiously expected. There seems little doubt that, if this armament had made Germany its object, Germany would at once have sprung to arms and have attempted, perhaps prematurely, what in 1813 it accomplished. What was expected in Germany had happened already in the Peninsula. Arthur Wellesley had landed at Lisbon on April 22, and in less than a month had driven Soult in confusion out of Portugal. In July he undertook an invasion of Spain by the valley of Tagus. Thus both the quantity and quality of resistance to Napoleon was greater than at any former time; but it was scattered, and the question was whether it could concentrate itself.

England was unfortunate this time in her intervention. The armament did not set sail till August, when in Austria the war seemed to be at an end, and when Wellesley, after winning the battle of Talavera, had seen himself obliged to retire into Portugal, and it was directed not to Germany but against Antwerp. It was therefore a mere diversion, and as such it proved unsuccessful. It created indeed a great flutter of alarm in the administration at Paris, which saw France itself left unprotected while its armies occupied Vienna and Madrid, but by mismanagement and misfortune the great enterprise failed, and accomplished nothing but the capture of Flushing.

And so the last triumph of Napoleon was achieved, and the treaty of Schönbrunn was signed on October 14. By this treaty, as by former treaties, he did not merely end a war or annex territory, but developed his empire and gave it a new character. He now brought to an end the duumvirate which had been established at Tilsit. Under that system his greatness had been dependent on the concert of Russia. He had had the czar's permission to seize Spain, the czar's cooperation in humbling Austria. Schönbrunn made his empire self-dependent and self-supporting, and thus in a manner completed the edifice. But he could not thus discard Russia without making her an enemy, and accordingly the Russian war appears on the horizon at the very moment that the Austrian war is terminated. This transformation was accomplished by first humbling Austria, and then, as it were, adopting her and giving her a favored place in the European confederacy. She lost population to the amount of 3,500,000, besides her access to the sea; she paid an indemnity of more than £3,000,000, and engaged to reduce her army to 150,000. But, thus humbled, a high and unique honor was reserved for her. We cannot be quite certain whether it was part of Napoleon's original plan to claim the hand of an archduchess, though this seems likely, since Napoleon would hardly break with Russia unless he felt secure of the alliance of Austria, and yet in the treaty of Schönbrunn he does not hesitate to offend Russia by raising the Polish question. What is certain is that after his return to France Napoleon proceeded at once to the divorce; that at the same time he asked the czar for the hand of his sister; that upon this Austria, alarmed, and seeing her own doom in the Russian match, gave him to understand (as he may very well have calculated that she would do) that he might have an archduchess; and that upon this he extricated himself from his engagement to the czar with a rudeness which might seem intended to make him an enemy. At the same time he refused to enter into an engagement not to raise the Polish question. We can understand the alarm of Austria, for the Russian match would perhaps have riveted most firmly the chains of Germany. In Napoleon's conduct reappears the same peculiarity that he had shown in his treatment of Prussia and of Spain. It seems less like statesmanship than some malignant vice of nature that he always turns upon an ally, even an ally who is most necessary to him. The sudden turn he now took, apparently without any necessity, involved him in the Russian expedition, and caused his ruin.

At an earlier period we saw Napoleon urged by his brothers to divorce Josephine, but refusing steadfastly and apparently resolved upon adopting the eldest son of Louis and Hortense. He had now quite ceased to be influenced by his brothers, but at the same time he had risen to such greatness that he had himself come to think differently of the question. Fourteen years before he had been warmly attached to Josephine; this attachment had been an effective feature in the character of republican hero which he then sustained. Mme. de Staël had been profoundly struck, when, on being charged by her with not liking women, he had answered, 'J'aime la mienne.' 'It was such an answer,' she said, 'as Epaminondas would have given!' He is now equally striking in the part of an Oriental sultan, and when he discards his Josephine from motives of ambition he requires to be publicly flattered for his self-sacrifice by the officials, by Josephine herself, and even by her son Eugène Beauharnais!

The archduchess Marie Louise, who now ventured to take the seat of Marie Antoinette, seems to have been of amiable but quite insignificant character. Her letters are childlike. She became a complete Frenchwoman, but, owing to a certain reserve of manner, was never specially popular.

On March 20, 1811, she bore a son, who took the title of King of Rome, by which in the Holy Roman Empire the successor had been designated. France had thus become once more as monarchical as in the proudest days of Versailles; but the child of empire was reserved for what his father called ' the saddest of fates, the fate of Astyanax.'

§ 3. *Annexation of Holland and Westphalia.* — *Dissolution of the alliance of Tilsit.* — *Invasion of Russia.*

Arrived now at the pinnacle, Napoleon pauses, as he had paused after Marengo. We are disposed to ask, What use will he now make of his boundless power ? It was a question he never considered, because the object he had set before himself in 1803 was not yet attained; he was not in the least satiated, because, much as he had gained, he had not gained what he sought, that is, the humiliation of England. As after Tilsit, so after Schönbrunn, he only asks, How may the new resources be best directed against England? Yet he did not, as we might expect, devote himself to crushing the resistance of the Peninsula. This he seems to have regarded with a mixed feeling of contempt and despair, not knowing how to overcome it, and persuading himself that it was not worth a serious effort. He persisted in saying that the only serious element in the Spanish opposition was the English army; this would fall with England herself; and England, he thought, was on the point of yielding to the blockade of the Continental system. He devotes himself henceforth therefore to heightening the rigor of this blockade. From the beginning it had led to continual annexations, because only Napoleon's own administration could be trusted to carry it into effect. Accordingly the two years 1810–11 witness a series of annexations chiefly on the northern sea-coast of Europe, where it was important to make the blockade more efficient. But on this northern sea-coast lay the chief interests of Russia. As therefore in 1805 he had brought Austria and Russia on himself by attacking England, so in 1810 he presses his hostility to England to the point that it breaks the alliance of Tilsit and leads to a Russian war.

The year 1810 is occupied with this heightening of the Continental system and the annexations which it involved. That he had long contemplated the annexation of Holland appears from the offer of the crown of Spain which he made to Louis in 1808, and the language he then used ('La Hollande ne saura sortir de ses ruines'). He now took advantage of the resistance which Louis made to his ruinous exactions. Louis was driven to abdicate, and the country was organized in nine French departments (July 9). In August the troops of the king of Westphalia were forced to make way for French troops at the mouths of the Elbe and Weser, and a few months later the whole coast between the Rhine and the Elbe was annexed. At the same time Napoleon began to make war on neutral commerce, especially American, affirming that in order to complete the destruction of English trade it was only necessary to prohibit it when it made use of neutral bottoms. So thoroughly in earnest was he with his Continental system; and indeed it is beyond dispute that great distress and discontent, nay, at last a war with the United States, were inflicted upon England by this policy.

But the pressure of it was felt even more on the Continent, and the ultimate cause of the fall of Napoleon was this, that under the weight of the Continental system the alliance of Tilsit broke down sooner than the resistance of England. That alliance had been seriously weakened by the Austrian marriage, and by Napoleon's refusal to give the guarantees which Russia required that Poland should never be restored. Indeed, Napoleon had seemed to take pleasure in weakening it, but perhaps he had only desired to make it less burdensome to himself without destroying it. At the end of 1810 measures were taken on both sides which conveyed the impression to Europe that it was practically at an end. Alexander refused to adopt Napoleon's policy towards neutrals; Napoleon answered by annexing Oldenburg, ruled by a Duke of the Russian house; Alexander rejoined by an ukase (December 31st) which modified the restrictions on colonial trade and heightened those on French trade.

In 1811 the alliance of Tilsit gradually dissolves. Napoleon's Russian expedition should not be regarded as an isolated freak of insane pride. He himself regarded it as the unfortunate effect of a fatality, and he betrayed throughout an unwonted reluctance and perplexity. 'The war must take place,' he said, 'it lies in the nature of things.' That is, it arose naturally, like the other Napoleonic wars, out of the quarrel with England. Upon the Continental system he had staked everything. He had united all Europe in the crusade against England, and no state, least of all such a state as Russia, could withdraw from the system without practically joining England. Nevertheless, we may wonder that, if he felt obliged to make war on Russia, he should have chosen to wage it in the manner he did, by an overwhelming invasion. For an ordinary war his resources were greatly superior to those of Russia. A campaign on the Lithuanian frontier would no doubt have been unfavorable to Alexander, and might have forced him to concede the points at issue. Napoleon had already experienced in Spain the danger of rousing national spirit. It seems, however, that this lesson had been lost on him, and that he still lived in the ideas which the campaigns of 1805, 1806, and 1807 had awakened, when he had occupied Vienna and Berlin in succession, overthrown the Holy Roman Empire, and conquered Prussia. He makes a dispute about tariffs the ground for the greatest military expedition known to authentic history! In this we see a stroke of his favorite policy, which consisted in taking with great suddenness a measure far more decisive than had been expected; but such policy seems here to have been wholly out of place. He was perhaps partly driven to it by the ill success of his diplomacy. War with France meant for Russia, sooner or later, alliance with England, but Napoleon was not able to get the help of Turkey, and Sweden joined Russia. Turkey had probably heard of the partition-schemes which were agitated at Tilsit, and was also influenced by the threats and promises of England. Sweden suffered grievously from the Continental system, and Bernadotte, who had lately become crown-prince, and who felt that he could only secure his position by procuring for Sweden some compensation for the recent loss of Finland, offered his adhesion to the power which would help him in acquiring Norway. Napoleon declined to rob his ally, Denmark, but Alexander made the promise, and Sweden was won. Against Russia, Sweden, and England (a coalition which formed itself but tardily) Napoleon assembled the forces of France, Italy, and Germany, and hoped to win, as usual, by the rapid concentration of an overwhelming force. Austria and Prussia had suffered so much in the former wars of the period, and especially in 1805-7, from the insincere and delusive alliance of Russia, that they were driven this time to side at least nominally with Napoleon. The army with which he invaded Russia consisted of somewhat more than 600,000 men, — the French troops mainly commanded by Davoust, Oudinot, and Ney, the Italian troops by Prince Eugene, the Poles by Poniatowski, the Austrian contingent (33,000 men) by Schwarzenberg, the remaining German troops by Gouvion St. Cyr, Reynier, Vandamme, Victor, Macdonald (who had the Prussian contingent), and Augereau. When we consider that the war of the Peninsula was at the same time at its height, and that England was now at war with the United States, we may form a notion of the calamitous condition of the world.

Russia had been defeated at Austerlitz and Friedland, where it fought far from home for a cause in which it was but slightly interested. Against an invasion it was as invincible as Spain, being strengthened by a profoundly national religion and perfect loyalty to the government; in addition it had the strength of its vast extent, its rigorous climate, and the half-nomad habits of its people. By his prodigious preparations Napoleon provoked a new national war under the most difficult circumstances, and yet he appears to have desired peace, and to have advanced most reluctantly. His campaign runs the same course as against Austria in 1805 and 1809. There is the successful advance, the capture of the fortress (Smolensk), the great victory (at Borodino), the entry into the capital (Moscow); but of all this no result. No negotiation follows, and Napoleon suddenly finds himself helpless, as perhaps he would have done in 1805 and 1809 had the enemy shown the same firmness.

§ 4. *Battle of Borodino. — Burning of Moscow. — Retreat from Moscow.*

On May 16, 1812, he arrived with Marie Louise at Dresden, where for the last time he appeared as king of kings — the Emperor of Austria, the King of Prussia, a multitude of German sovereigns, Metternich and Hardenberg paying court to him. On the 28th he set out again, and travelled by Glogau, Thorn, Dantzic, Königsberg, Gumbinnen, to Vilkowyski, where he arrived on June 21st. On the 24th the mass of the army passed the Niemen at Kovno, and on the 28th Napoleon entered Vilna, which was evacuated by the Russians. Here he remained till July 16th. In this long delay, as well as in other circumstances, the unwonted perplexity of his mind appears. Alexander, who has by this time gained greatly in decision of character, refuses to negotiate while the enemy stands on Russian territory; Napoleon, in conversation with Balacheff, shows an almost pathetic desire for an amicable arrangement. He is embarrassed again when a deputation from Warsaw, where a diet had met, bids him only say that '*Poland exists*, since his decree would be for the world equivalent to the reality.' This word he declines to say, alleging his obligations to Austria. From his conversations with Narbonne (Villemain, *Souvenirs*) we find that he had deliberately considered and rejected what we may call the rational mode of waging war with Russia, that is, through the restoration of Poland. He admitted that he might indemnify Austria, and, if necessary, Prussia elsewhere, but he argued that he could not afford to open the floodgates of republicanism: 'Poland must be a camp, not a forum.' He had in fact — perhaps mainly since his second marriage — come to regard himself as the representative of legitimacy against the Revolution. It was thus with his eyes open that he preferred the fatal course of striking at Moscow. His judgment was evidently bewildered by the successes of 1805 and 1806, and he indulges in chimerical imaginations of delivering Europe once for all from the danger of barbaric invasion. It is to be observed that he seems invariably to think of the Russians as Tartars!

In relating this war we have to beware of national exaggerations on both sides. On Napoleon's side it is absurdly said that he was only vanquished by winter, whereas it is evident that he brought the winter upon himself, first by beginning so late, then by repeated delays, at Vilna, at Vitebsk, and most of all at Moscow. On the other side, we must not admit absolutely the Russian story that he was lured onward by a Parthian policy, and that Moscow was sacrificed by a solemn universal act of patriotism. Wellington's policy of retrograde movements had indeed come into fashion among specialists, and an entrenched camp was preparing at Drissa on the Dwina in imitation of Torres Vedras. But the nation and the army were full of reckless confidence and impatience for battle; only their preparations were by no means complete. The long retreat to Moscow and beyond it was unintentional, and filled the Russians with despair, while at the same time it agreed with the views of some of the more enlightened strategists.

As usual, Napoleon took the enemy by surprise, and brought an overwhelming force to the critical point. When he crossed the Niemen the Russians were still thinking of an offensive war, and rumors had also been spread that he would enter Volhynia. Hence their force was divided into three armies: one, commanded by the Livonian Barclay de Tolly, had its headquarters at Vilna; a second, under Prince Bagration, was further south at Volkowysk; the third, under Tormaseff, was in Volhynia. But the total of these armies scarcely amounted to 200,000 men, and that of Barclay de

Tolly opposed little more than 100,000 to the main body of Napoleon's host, which amounted nearly to 300,000. Hence it evacuates Vilna and retires by Svenziany to the camp at Drissa. Barclay arrives at Drissa on July 9th, and here for the first time the emperor and the generals seem to realize the extent of the danger. Alexander issues an ukase calling out the population in the proportion of five to every hundred males, and hurries to Moscow, and thence to St. Petersburg, in order to rouse the national enthusiasm. The Drissa camp is also perceived to be untenable. It had been intended to screen St. Petersburg, and Napoleon is seen to look rather in the direction of Moscow. Barclay retires to Vitebsk, but is obliged, in order to effect his junction with Bagration, to retreat still further, and Napoleon enters Vitebsk on the 28th. The road to Moscow passes between the Dwina, which flows northward, and the Dnieper, which flows southward, Vitebsk on the one river and Smolensk on the other, forming, as it were, the two doorposts. We expect to find Napoleon at this point cutting the hostile armies in two, and compelling that of Bagration to surrender; he has a great superiority of numbers, and he might have had the advantage of a friendly population. But his host seems unmanageable, and the people are estranged by the rapacity and cruelty to which it is driven by insufficient supplies. Barclay and Bagration effect their junction at Smolensk on August 3, and now have a compact army of at least 120,000 men. They evacuate Smolensk also on the 18th, but only after an obstinate defence, which left Napoleon master of nothing but a burning ruin.

Both at Vitebsk and Smolensk he betrayed the extreme embarrassment of his mind. Should he go into winter quarters? should he press forward to Moscow? It was a choice of desperate courses. His army was dwindling away; he had forfeited the support of the Poles; Germany was full of discontent; and yet a large part of his army was Polish or German; how could he delay? And yet if he advanced, since August was already running out, he must encounter the Russian winter. He determined to advance, relying on the overwhelming effect that would be produced by the occupation of Moscow. He would win, as after Austerlitz and Friedland, through the feebleness and fickleness of Alexander.

Meanwhile his unresisted progress, and the abandonment by Barclay of one position after another, created the greatest consternation among the Russians, as well they might. Barclay was a foreigner, and might well seem another Melas or Mack. A cry arose for his dismissal, to which the Czar responded by putting old Kutusoff, who was at least a Russian, at the head of all his armies. This change necessarily brought on a great battle, which took place on September 7, near the village of Borodino. More than 100,000 men with about six hundred pieces of artillery were engaged on each side. It ended in a victory, but an almost fruitless victory, for the French. They lost perhaps 30,000 men, including Generals Montbrun and Caulaincourt, the Russians nearly 50,000, including Prince Bagration. Here again Napoleon displayed unwonted indecision. He refused to let loose his guard, consisting of 20,000 fresh troops, who might apparently have effected the complete dissolution of the hostile army, and materially altered the whole sequel of the campaign. He said, 'At 800 leagues from Paris one must not risk one's last reserve.'

This battle, the greatest after Leipsic of all the Napoleonic battles, was followed by the occupation of Moscow on September 14, which, to Napoleon's great disappointment, was found almost entirely empty. After a council of war Kutusoff had taken the resolution to abandon the old capital, the loss of which was held not to be so irreparable as the loss of the army. But, as with Old-Russian craft he had announced Borodino to the Czar as a victory, the sensation produced upon the Russian public by the fall of Moscow was all the more overwhelming. Nor did the next occurrence, which immediately followed, at first bring any relief. Fires broke out in Moscow on the night after Napoleon's entrance; on the next night, by which time he was quartered in the Kremlin, the greater part of the city was in flames, and on the day following he was forced by the progress of the conflagration to evacuate the Kremlin again. But on the first intelligence of this catastrophe the destruction of Moscow was attributed in Russia to the French themselves, and was not by any means regarded as a crushing blow dealt at Napoleon by Russian patriotism.

It is indeed not clear that this event had any decisive influence upon the result of the war. Nor does it seem to have been the deliberate work of the patriotism of Moscow. The beginner of it was one man, Count Rostopchin, governor of Moscow, who is shown by many public utterances to have brooded for some time over the thought, and is proved to have made preparations for carrying it into effect before leaving the town. It is, however, supposed that what was begun by him was

completed by a rabble which had no object but
plunder, and partly by French soldiers. The immediate
effect of it was to deepen the alarm of
the Russians, and, when this feeling passed away,
to deepen their hatred of the French. Now came
the critical moment. Would Alexander negotiate?
That is, would he listen to certain timid courtiers
about him such as Romanzoff, or would he be inspired
by the partiotic ardor of his people and
lean on his nobler counsellors, the German patriot
Stein or Sir Robert Wilson? The pressure for a
moment was great. We can imagine that had the
Russian army been dissolved at Borodino, it might
have been irresistible. But he stood firm; he refused
to negotiate; and Napoleon suddenly found
that he had before him, not the simple problem
he had solved so often in earlier life, but the insoluble
puzzle he had first encountered in Spain.
His failures in Egypt and in Spain had been more
or less disguised. He was now in danger of a
failure which could not be concealed, and on a far
larger scale; but had he retreated forthwith and
wintered in Vilna, where he might have arrived
early in November, the conquest of Russia might
have seemed only to be postponed for a year. Instead
of this he delayed five weeks in Moscow,
and then complained of the Russian winter!

After planning a demonstration on St. Petersburg, weighing Daru's scheme of wintering in Moscow (which he called 'un conseil de lion'), and waiting in vain for the Czar's submission, he set out on October 20, after blowing up the Kremlin. He marched southward to Kaluga, hoping to make his way through a richer and unexhausted country. But while his forces had dwindled the Russian had increased. Peace with Sweden had released a Russian force in Finland; peace with Turkey released the army of the Danube; meanwhile levies were proceeding through the whole empire. Napoleon's plan was frustrated by a check he received at Malojaroslavetz, and he had to turn northward again and return as he had come. He reached Smolensk on November 9, when he might have been at Vilna. He marched by Orcza to the Berezina, which he struck near Borisoff. Here Tchitchagoff at the head of the Danube army confronted him, and two other Russian armies were approaching. Napoleon on his side was joined by what remained of the corps of Oudinot and Victor, who had held the line of the Dwina. But what was the army of Napoleon which was thus reinforced?

In July it had consisted of more than 250,000 men. It had suffered no decisive defeat, and yet it amounted now only to 12,000; in the retreat from Moscow alone about 90,000 had been lost. The force which now joined it amounted to 18,000, and Napoleon's star had still influence enough to enable him to make his way across the Berezina, and so escape total ruin and captivity. But December came on, and the cold was more terrible than ever. On the evening of December 6th a miserable throng, like a crowd of beggars, tottered into Vilna.

The corps of Macdonald, Reynier, and Schwarzenberg (among whom were included the Austrian and Prussian contingents) had escaped destruction, having been posted partly on the Polish frontier, partly in the Baltic provinces. For these we may deduct 100,000 from the total force; it then appears that half a million had perished or disappeared. They had perished not by unexpected cold; 'the cold had but finished the work of dissolution and death almost accomplished by the enemy, by hardship, and especially by hunger' (Charras); nor is cold unusual in Russia in November! Napoleon's error was one which may be traced as clearly in the campaigns of 1805 and 1806, the error of making no provision whatever for the case of ill-success or even success less than complete.

It was now the twentieth year that Europe was tearing itself to pieces. For some years past the pretence of revolutionary principles had been given up. There was now no pretext for war except the so-called maritime tyranny of England; but yet the magnitude of wars had increased beyond all measurement. The campaign of 1812 left everything in civilized history far behind it. All the abuses of the old monarchy and all the atrocities of the Revolution put together were as nothing compared to this new plague, bred between the Revolution and the old monarchy, having the violence of the one and the vainglory of the other, with a systematic professional destructiveness peculiar to imperialism superadded.

CHAPTER VI.

FALL OF NAPOLEON.

§ 1. *Wars of* 1813–14.—*War with Russia and Prussia.* — *Relations to Austria.*

BUT what was Napoleon's position! Any government but the strongest would have sunk under such a blow, but Napoleon's government was the strongest, and at its strongest moment. Opposition had long been dead; public opinion was paralyzed; no immediate rising was to be feared. Should he then simply take the lesson home, and make peace with Alexander? Impossible; he must efface the disaster by new triumphs. But, as this was evident to all, Alexander could not but perceive that he must not lose a moment, but must hasten forward and rouse Germany, before Napoleon should have had time to levy a new army. 1813 must be filled with a war in Germany, as 1812 with the war in Russia.

Napoleon abandoned the wreck of his army at Smorgoni on December 5 (as he had left his Egyptian army thirteen years before), travelling in a carriage placed upon a sledge, and accompanied by Caulaincourt and Duroc. He had an interview with Maret outside Vilna, and then travelled to Warsaw, where he saw his ambassador De Pradt, who has left an account of his confused talk. Here, as in the famous 29th bulletin, published a little later, we observe that he consoles himself for the loss of his army by reflecting that his own health was never better — he kept on repeating this. Then he said, 'From the sublime to the ridiculous there is but a step;' for the retreat from Moscow strikes him as *ridiculous!* From Warsaw he passed to Dresden, where he saw his ally the King of Saxony, and wrote letters to the Emperor of Austria and to the King of Prussia. He then made his way by Erfurt and Mainz to Paris, where he arrived on December 18th. The bulletin had appeared two days before.

He had said to De Pradt that he intended to raise 300,000 men and appear on the Niemen again in the spring. The first part of this intention he fulfilled, for in April he reappeared in the field with 300,000 men; but the campaign was fought not on the line of the Niemen, nor of the Vistula, nor of the Oder, and he had to fight a battle before he could even reach the Elbe. For a great event took place less than a fortnight after his arrival in Paris, the defection of the Prussian contingent under York from the grand army; this event led to the rising of Prussia against Napoleon. York's convention with the Russians is dated December 30th. On January 22, 1813, Stein appeared at Königsberg and procured the assembling of the estates of East Prussia, in which assembly the Prussian landwehr was set on foot. On February 27th he concluded for the Czar the treaty of Kalisch with Prussia, by which the old Coalition of 1806 may be said to have been revived. Prussia now rushed to arms in a wholly new spirit, emulating Spain and Russia in devotion, and adding to devotion an intelligence peculiar to herself. At the same time measures were taken to break up the Confederation of the Rhine. Tettenborn cleared the French out of the northern departments in March; Saxony too passed into the hands of the allies, and it was hoped that the king himself might be induced to follow the example of the King of Prussia. But April came, and Napoleon took the field again.

By rapidity and energy he was still able to take the offensive. Though Russia and Prussia were now as Spain, yet the process of calling out and drilling their population was only just begun, and it proceeded slowly. Their united available force at the opening of the campaign scarcely exceeded 100,000 men. Austria and the middle states did not abandon Napoleon. With tact and with judicious concession he might yet retrieve his position; perhaps no one as yet had begun to think of his fall. He left St. Cloud for Mainz on April 15th. His object was Saxony, where Dresden, the scene of his last display of omnipotence less than a year ago, was now the residence of the Czar and the King of Prussia united against him. Eugene was maintaining himself on the lower Saale with an army of about 70,000 men, and Napoleon was to march by way of Erfurt to join him. Between Erfurt, Bamberg, and Mainz he had by this time about 150,000 men, troops indeed without discipline and with imperfect drill, youths, the last hope of France, but well officered and not wanting in the enthusiasm which his name still inspired. There was, however, a serious deficiency of cavalry. Meanwhile Davoust, stationed on the Weser with 30,000 men, was holding down the insurrection of North Germany.

The war which now commenced ended not only to the disadvantage of Napoleon, but, unlike any former war, it ended in a complete defeat of France, nay, in the conquest of France, an event to which nothing parallel had been seen in modern Europe. Nor was this result attained by any political or revolutionary means, *e.g.*, by exciting a republican or Bourbon party against Napoleon's authority, but by sheer military superiority. The great conqueror was in his turn completely conquered.

This strange reverse seems traceable to two principal causes.

(1) He had lost in Russia the unparalleled army, which had been bequeathed to him by the Revolution, and which had been the instrument of his military achievements.

(2) He had succeeded in uniting against himself Austria, Russia, and Prussia. Upon the incurable mutual distrust of these three Powers the greatness of France during the whole period had been based. This had driven Prussia from the first coalition, and held her aloof from the second and third. Moreover, the treacherous policy initiated by Catharine at the outset had passed to Alexander, and had been blended in him with characteristic frivolity. He had ruined Austria in 1805 and Prussia in 1806 by this mixture of frivolity

and treachery. In 1807 he had gone openly over to the enemy, and between 1807 and 1812 the German Powers had been held in subjection as much by him as by Napoleon. Napoleon's insensate blindness had flung away this strong support, and had achieved what might have seemed impossible — had united the three Powers in a cordial alliance. In place of the old bitterness towards Prussia there now reigned in Austria the conviction, which Metternich was fond of expressing, that the restoration of Prussia was a vital Austrian interest, and it had become equally clear to Russia that the restoration of Austria and Prussia was necessary to her.

The war, though technically one, is really three distinct wars. There is first the war with Russia and Prussia, which occupies the month of May and is concluded by an armistice on June 4th. There is next a war with Russia, Prussia, and Austria, which begins in August and is practically terminated in October by the expulsion of Napoleon from Germany. Thirdly, there is an invasion of France by the same allied powers. This began in January, 1814, and ended in April with the fall of Napoleon.

In the first of these wars Napoleon maintained on the whole his old superiority. It has excited needless admiration that with his raw levies he should still have been able to win victories, since of his two enemies Russia had suffered as much as himself in 1812, and Prussia's army was at the beginning of the year actually to make. In the first days of May he advanced down the valley of the Saale, making for Leipsic by Naumburg, Weissenfels, and Lützen. On the 2d was fought the battle commonly called from Lützen, though the Germans usually name it from the village of Gross-Görschen. By this battle, in which the great military reformer of Prussia, Scharnhorst, received the wound of which he died soon after, the allies were forced to retreat across the Elbe, and Dresden was restored to the King of Saxony. The Prussians attribute their ill-success partly to the insufficiency of the Russian commander Wittgenstein, under whom they fought. Napoleon soon pursued the allies across the Elbe, and another battle was fought on May 20 and 21 at Bautzen on the Spree. Here again Napoleon remained master of the field, though his loss seems to have been considerably greater than that of the enemy. The allies retired into Silesia, and a pause took place, which led to the armistice of Poischwitz, signed on June 4th. During this armistice Napoleon formed the resolution which led to his downfall.

He might seem now to have almost retrieved his losses. If he could not revive the great army of the Revolution, which lay buried (or unburied) in Russia, he had reasserted the ascendency of France. Politically he had suffered but one substantial loss, in the rebellion of Prussia. The blows of Lützen and Bautzen had arrested the movement which threatened to dissolve the Confederation of the Rhine and to unite all Germany against him. They had also shaken the alliance of Prussia and Russia. Between the generals of the two armies there reigned much jealousy; the old question, raised after Austerlitz and Friedland, was beginning to be asked again by the Russians, Why should they fight for others?

At Tilsit Napoleon had dissolved the Coalition by forming as it were a partnership with Russia. It might seem possible now to form a similar partnership with Austria. This course had indeed been entered upon at the marriage of the archduchess. Napoleon seems to have taken the alliance seriously. He conceived it as the final suppression of the Revolution, as a complete adhesion on his own part to conservatism. The language of the bulletins at this time is ultra-conservative. Thus the enemy is described as 'preaching anarchy and insurrection.' Stein is

charged with 'rousing the rabble against the
proprietors.' But though he had borrowed the
Austrian tone, he had not yet enlisted Austrian
interests on his side. It was evidently in his
power to confer on Austria the greatest advantages, and, as it were, to divide his power with
her. Less than this he could not offer, since the
losses of France and Russia had given to Austria
a decisive weight, but it might seem that he could
offer it without much humiliation, as the alliance
with Austria had subsisted since 1810 and had
been cemented by marriage. If he did not thus
win Austria, he might expect her to adhere to the
other side, for in such a crisis neutrality was out
of the question. Could Napoleon then hope to
overcome a quadruple alliance of England, Russia, Prussia, and Austria? Such a hope was not
justified by the victories of Lützen and Bautzen.
The force of Prussia increased every day, and the
Spanish enthusiasm with which her new army
fought had been displayed even on those fields;
the force of Austria had been impaired by no
Russian campaign; while France was evidently
near the end of her resources. The legerdemain
by which, in 1800, 1805, 1806, Napoleon had
made conquests was now worn out; his blows
were no longer followed by abject submission

and surrender; he was not even able, for want of cavalry, to make his victories decisive. Thus ample concessions to Austria were indispensable; but, these assumed, his position might seem hopeful.

He took the momentous resolution to make no such concessions, saw Austria join the Coalition, and after a campaign of two months found his army driven in tumultuous ruin across the Rhine. This step is the counterpart of Tilsit, and destroyed the work of Tilsit. To understand it we must in the first place weigh his own words, spoken to Schwarzenberg: 'My situation is difficult; I should ruin myself if I concluded a dishonorable peace. An old government, where the ties between sovereign and people are old, may sign burdensome conditions, when the pressure of circumstances requires it. But I am new; I must heed opinion more, for I need it. Were such a peace announced, at first, no doubt, we should hear nothing but jubilation; but soon would follow loud criticism on the Government. I should lose the respect, and with that the confidence, of my people, for the Frenchman has a lively imagination; he loves glory and excitement; he is sensitive. Do you know what was the first cause of the fall of the Bourbons? It dates from Rossbach.' This view is evidently sound, but it does not explain why he did not at least try his utmost by bribes and promises to win Austria to his interest. Nevertheless he seems not to have been attracted by this plan, though it was open to him for several months, and though the clamor for peace which his own army and his own marshals raised compelled him to profess to take it into consideration. He continued deliberately to contemplate in preference a war against Russia, Prussia, and Austria united, and regarded the armistice simply as a delay, which would enable him to bring up new forces. Metternich has left us an account of the interview, lasting ten hours, which he had with Napoleon on June 28, in the Marcolini palace at Dresden. It reveals to us Napoleon's contempt for a power he has so often defeated, his inability to believe that Austria can still have spirit to resist; at the same time we become aware that he believes himself to be necessary to the Austrian emperor, as being the bulwark of all thrones and of monarchy itself against the Revolution. Here too we meet with the famous dramatic passage, which we can hardly suppose to have been invented by Metternich, where Napoleon, on being told that his troops were 'not soldiers, but children,' answered, turning pale — 'You are no soldier; you do not know what passes in a soldier's mind; I grew up in the field, and a man like me troubles himself little about the life of a million of men' (the actual expression he used, adds Metternich, cannot be reported),—and then flung his hat into a corner of the room. That this was a true description of his way of thinking had become visible to most since the Russian catastrophe, and the audacious frankness with which he blurts it out is quite in his characteristic manner.

We cannot but feel how difficult it is to follow the movements of a mind which has wandered into such strange latitudes. His judgment, too, which was naturally most correct, must have been bewildered by the strangeness of his career. He must have formed the habit of counting upon sudden interventions of fortune; nay, he must have been well aware that he had risen so high not by following probabilities, but by running enormous risks.

But it is by no means certain, after all, that Austria was to be bought or bribed. Her course, so far as we can trace it, was firm and honorable; it seems that the sacrifice of the Archduchess in 1809 ought not to be regarded as Austria's final surrender of self-respect. She quietly withdraws her auxiliary corps from the French army, and takes up the position of a mediator, arming vigorously to sustain this position. She then offers terms. By accepting these Napoleon would have conciliated her, and he would have gained time, perhaps he would have gained much more — for instance, an army of veteran troops still shut up in Prussian fortresses. But he would not have purchased an immediate peace at this price.

A congress met at Prague in the course of July, but Napoleon did not allow its deliberations to make serious progress. He paid no attention to an ultimatum presented on August 8, which consisted of six principal conditions. (1) Partition of the Duchy of Warsaw between Austria, Prussia, and Russia, (2) restitution to Prussia of Dantzig and its territory, (3) cession of the Illyrian provinces to Austria, (4) restoration to independence of Hamburg and Lubeck, and arrangement of the 32d Military Division, (5) dissolution of the Confederation of the Rhine, (6) reconstitution of Prussia on the scale of 1806. On midnight of August 10–11 the armistice was declared to be at an end, and the doom of Napoleon was sealed. It was a strange decision on his part, but perhaps he judged rightly that he had no choice but between ruin and absolute, impossible victory.

§ 2. *War with Russia, Prussia, and Austria.*

Europe now plunges again into a struggle as desperate and as destructive as that of 1812. More evidently even than in 1812 is Napoleon responsible for this ruin of all civilization. He cannot any longer speak even of the liberty of the seas, for he is forced himself to admit that the Continental system is dead, and yet refuses to surrender that ascendency for which the Continental system had all along been the pretext. Infatuated France, however, has by this time furnished more than 400,000 men to perish in a contest where there might be chances, but could be no probability, of victory. His head-quarters are now at Dresden, and his armies are arranged along the whole course of the Elbe from Bohemia to its mouth. This position has been somewhat weakened by the adhesion of Austria to the Coalition, for Austria masses her troops on the north-west of Bohemia, threatening Dresden and Napoleon's communications from the left side of the Elbe. The forces of the allies (approaching 500,000 men) consists of three great armies, of which the first, principally Austrian, and commanded by Prince Schwarzenberg, is stationed on the Eger in Bohemia; the sovereigns are here. The old Prusso-

Russian army, which had made the convention of
Poischwitz, is still in Silesia. It contains more
Russians than Prussians, but a Prussian officer is
now put at the head of it. This is Blücher, the
dashing general of hussars, now an old man of
seventy years; on his staff are some of the leading theorists and enthusiasts of the new Prussian
army, such as Gneisenau. But the bulk of the
Prussian force is stationed in the Mark of Bran-
denburg. In this final muster of the armies of
Europe we see that the moral forces have passed
over from France to the allies. In the French
camp there reigns weariness and desire for peace,
among the Prussians and Russians heroic ardor
and devotion. But the old mismanagement reappears on the side of the allies. In the Bohemian
camp Schwarzenberg's authority was almost annulled by the presence of the sovereigns; in Silesia the heroic Prussian general is in command
of an army mainly Russian. But in the Mark
perhaps the greatest blunder was made, for here
the main Prussian force was put under the orders
of the Crown Prince of Sweden, the Frenchman
Bernadotte, wholly alien to the German cause, and
bent upon propitiating French public opinion with
a view to the succession of Napoleon. Bernadotte
is not the only member of the old republican

opposition who is seen in the allied camp, now that Napoleon's fall begins to be thought of as possible. Moreau, the man who helped in 1799 to found the consulate, desiring probably to see France ruled by a series of Washingtons, each holding office for a short term, appears in the Austrian camp. If Napoleon was to be dethroned, who had better right to succeed him?

The campaign opens with a blow aimed at Berlin, where perhaps Napoleon wished to extinguish the popular insurrection at its source. Oudinot marches on it from Baruth, and is supported by a force from Magdeburg; Davoust sends another corps from Hamburg. Bernadotte proposes to retire and sacrifice Berlin, but in spite of him Bülow fights on August 23 the battle of Grossbeeren, within a few miles of the capital. Here first the landwehr distinguished itself, and Berlin was saved. The attack from Magdeburg was defeated by Hirschfeld at Hagelberg on the 27th. Meanwhile Napoleon himself, at the head of 150,000 men, had marched against Blücher on the Katzbach. Blücher retired before him, and he was compelled to return to the defence of Dresden, but he left Macdonald with perhaps 50,000 or 60,000 men to hold Blücher in check. Almost immediately after his departure (August 26) Macdonald was defeated by Blücher in the battle of the Katzbach. Thus the campaign began with two Prussian victories. But when the great army of Bohemia moved upon Dresden, Napoleon showed his old superiority. On August 27 he inflicted on it a terrible defeat. Here Moreau, the hero of Hohenlinden, was mortally wounded by a cannon-ball. It seemed for a moment likely that this battle, followed up with Napoleon's overwhelming rapidity, would decide the campaign. He prepared to cut off his enemy's retreat into Bohemia. But the news of Grossbeeren and Katzbach arrived; Napoleon is also said to have been attacked by illness; he altered his plan in the moment of execution. The grand stroke of the campaign failed, and, instead of cutting off the retreat of the grand army, Vandamme was taken prisoner with 10,000 men at Kulm after a battle in which he had lost half that number (August 30). It was evident that the times of Marengo and Austerlitz were over. Napoleon's ability and authority were as great as ever; he controlled larger armies; he opposed a Coalition which was as unwieldy as former Coalitions; and yet he had suffered four defeats in a single week and had won but one victory. Within another week he suffered another blow. Ney, making a new advance on Berlin, was defeated with great loss at Dennewitz by the Prussians under Bülow (September 6).

Here then ends Napoleon's ascendency; henceforth he fights in self-defence or in despair. Yet the massacre was to continue with unabated fury for nearly two months longer. He spent the greater part of September in restless marches from Dresden, now into Silesia, now into Bohemia, by which he wore out his strength without winning any substantial advantage. Towards the end of the month a new phase of the war begins. From the beginning the allies had given each other rendezvous in the plain of Leipsic. Hitherto Napoleon had held the line of the Elbe, and had presented a single mass to the three separate armies of the Coalition. Now that his collapse begins to be visible, commences the converging advance on Leipsic. The Silesian army crossed the Elbe at Wartenburg on October 3, and on the next days the northern army also crossed at several points. At the same moment the Confederation of the Rhine began rapidly to dissolve. A troop of Cossacks under Czernicheff upset the kingdom of Westphalia (October 1). Bavaria abandoned Napoleon, and concluded the treaty of Ried with Austria (October 8). But for form's sake — we may almost say — a final massacre was still necessary. It took place on a satisfactory scale between October 14 and 19, and ended in the decisive defeat of Napoleon and the capture of Leipsic. Perhaps nearly half a million of men were engaged in these final battles. It is reckoned that in the last three days the Prussians lost sixteen, the Russians twenty-one, and the Austrians fourteen thousand men — total, fifty-one thousand. Napoleon left twenty-three thousand behind him in the hospitals, and fifteen thousand prisoners; his dead may have been fifteen thousand. He lost also three hundred pieces of artillery. The sufferings of the wounded almost exceed anything told of the retreat from Moscow. It is a misfortune that the victors allowed him to cross the Rhine in safety; had they pressed the pursuit vigorously, helped as they now were by the Bavarians, they might have brought his career to an end at this point. But for such a decisive measure perhaps even their political views were not yet ripe. However, as at the Berezina in 1812, so now, he had to clear his road by another battle. The Bavarians under Wrede met him at Hanau, eager to earn some merit with the victorious Coalition; but he broke his way through them (October 30, 31), and arrived at Frankfort. On November 1, 2, he carried the remains of his army, some 70,000 men, across the Rhine at Mainz.

§ 3. *Invasion of France by the Allies.* — *Napoleon abdicates.*

The work of eight years was undone; Napoleon was thrown back to the position he had occupied at the rupture of the peace of Amiens. The Russian disaster had cancelled Friedland; Leipsic had cancelled Austerlitz. But could Napoleon consent to humble himself? If he could not make concessions in the summer, still less could he do so now. Could he return and reign quietly at Paris, a defeated general, his reputation crushed by the two greatest disasters of history? At least he might by abdicating have spared France, already mortally exhausted, the burden of another war. It is among the most unpardonable even of his crimes to have dragged his unhappy country through yet another period of massacre, though nothing that could even appear to be a national interest was at stake. In November advances were made to him by the allies, in which peace was proposed on the basis of the 'natural frontiers.' This would have secured to France the main fruits of the First Revolutionary War, that is, Belgium, the Left Bank, Savoy, and Nice. Such terms seem generous when we consider the prostration of France, and the overwhelming superiority of the allies. But though the Prussian war-party loudly protested against them, and maintained the necessity of weakening France so as to render her harmless, Austria favored them, being jealous alike of Prussia and of the spirit of liberty which the war was rousing in the German population. A little compliance on the part of Napoleon might at this moment have made the general desire for peace irresistible. But he showed no such disposition. He first evaded the proposal, and then, too late, accepted it with suspicious qualifications. After having been decimated, France must now be invaded and subjugated, for him.

On December 1 the allies issued their manifesto from Frankfort, in which they declare themselves at war not with France but with Napoleon (an imitation of the Revolutionary principle 'Peace with peoples, war with Governments'), and the invasion followed with almost Napoleonic rapidity. The three armies remain separate as they had been in Germany. The great army under Schwarzenberg passes through Switzerland, and makes its way to the plateau of Langres (the source of the Seine, Aube, and Marne), where it begins to arrive about the middle of January; Blücher's Silesian army crosses the middle Rhine to Nancy; the northern army, nominally under Bernadotte, passes through Holland. In the course of the march Switzerland and Holland were swept into the Coalition, the resources of which now became overwhelming. It would be difficult to state for what object Napoleon called on France to fight another campaign, particularly as the allies guaranteed to her a larger territory than she had possessed under the old monarchy. His officers indeed wondered what personal object he could have. They were astonished to hear him talk of another campaign in Germany to be undertaken next spring, of being soon on the Vistula again, &c. He was no doubt a prey to illusions, his fortune having accustomed him to expect results ten times greater than the probabilities justified, but his confidence was founded on (1) the great force which still remained to him shut up in German fortresses, (2) the mutual jealousy of the allies, (3) his own connection with the Emperor of Austria, (4) the patriotism which would be roused among the French, as in 1792, by the invasion. But his calculations were confounded by the rapidity of the invaders, who gave him no time to call out the nation. The Senate did indeed grant him 300,000 men, but to levy, drill, and arm them was impossible, and he had neglected to fortify Paris. In the armies which had returned from Germany there began desertion of all who were not French. The campaign opened at the end of January, and was over at the end of March. The scene of it was the country between the Marne, Aube, and Seine, partly also the department of Aisne. At first, though successful at Brienne, Napoleon seemed unable to resist the superior numbers of the enemy. He was defeated at La Rothière. But the invaders were as yet irresolute; they divided their forces. This gave him an opportunity. He attacked Blücher, and, though with greatly inferior forces, won four battles in four days, at Champaubert (February 10), at Montmirail (11), at Chateau-Thierry (12), at Vauchamps (13). For the moment this brilliant success gave the campaign quite another character; the hopes and patriotic feelings of the French were roused. A congress had already been opened at Châtillon, and under the impression of these victories it would have been easy to conclude a peace, had not Napoleon's position made a reasonable peace inadmissible to him. He felt this, and fell back upon illusions, and upon attempts to sever Austria from the Coalition. At the beginning of March the Coalition was strengthened by the treaty of Chaumont, in which each of the four powers bound themselves for twenty years to keep

150,000 men on foot. Directly afterwards Napoleon received a crushing blow from the fall of Soissons and the junction of Blücher's army with the northern army under Bülow, which had entered France by way of Holland and Belgium. Their united force amounted to more than 100,000 men. The battles of Craonne and Laon followed, in which Napoleon, without suffering actual defeat, saw his resources dwindle away. On March 18 the conferences at Châtillon came to an end, the plenipotentiaries of the allies declaring Napoleon to have no intention but that of gaining time. About the 24th the allies came to the resolution to march on Paris. They had before them only Marmont and Mortier, for Napoleon himself had resolved to manœuvre in their rear, and had marched to St. Dizier. The marshals, after an engagement at Fère Champenoise, made good their retreat to Paris, where the enemy followed them on the 29th. Joseph Bonaparte withdrew Marie Louise and the King of Rome to Tours. On the 30th the allies attacked in three divisions — the Silesian army on the side of Montmartre, Prince Eugene of Würtemberg and Barclay de Tolly by Pantin and Romainville, the Crown Prince of Würtemberg and Giulay by Vincennes and Charenton. In the afternoon, after an obstinate resistance, the marshals offered a capitulation, and engaged to evacuate the town before seven o'clock in the morning. Napoleon, advancing by forced marches, was too late. The military struggle is over; the political struggle begins.

Since 1804 there had been no independent political life in France. During the Russian expedition, indeed, a certain General Malet had spread a false report of Napoleon's death in Russia, and had produced a forged decree of the Senate restoring the republic. His attempt had for the moment had so much success that Napoleon had painfully felt the precariousness of his dynasty, the purely provisional character of the monarchy he had founded. Lainé of Bordeaux again had been bold enough, when Napoleon made his last appeal for help to the Corps Législatif, to conjure him, while he defended the country, to maintain the entire execution of the laws which guarantee to the citizen liberty, security, and property, and to the nation the free exercise of its political rights. Napoleon had replied with an outburst of indignation. But now at last it became necessary to take an independent resolution, for in the influential classes it began to be understood that Napoleon must fall, and in particular the generals asked themselves for what rational purpose troops were still levied and battles still fought. But not even the germs were visible of any authority that could replace that of Napoleon. Should he be succeeded by another general, or by a regency for his son, or by the Bourbons? The first course might have been possible had some Moreau been at hand; even as it was, Bernadotte, who, like Napoleon, was a Jacobin developed into a prince, made pretensions which were favored by the Czar. Such a course would have been a revival of the consulate, but it would not have satisfied the republican party, while it would have been rejected by monarchists of every shade. In favor of the regency, as against the Bourbons, there was much to be said. It would not begin with a fantastic transformation-scene, and it would have a hold on the popular imagination. The decision fell out by a sort of accident. To a regency the natural road was by an abdication, which would preserve the principle of inheritance. Such an abdication Napoleon gave. On April 4th he reviewed his troops at Fontainebleau, and announced his intention of attacking the allies in Paris. They received his words with enthusiasm; but just at this point the mainstay of his power failed him. The military aristocracy, the marshals, refused to follow him, and Napoleon recognized in a moment that the end was come. Though in arguing with them he had said that a regency of Marie Louise, whom he called 'a child,' was impossible, yet he now abdicated on condition that his son should succeed under the regency of the empress. Ney, Macdonald, and Caulaincourt set out for Paris to negotiate the establishment of the regency.

Napoleon's power rested first on the support of the great military magnates, but secondly on that of the great civil dignitaries, lavishly enriched by him, whose organ was the Senate. While the marshals forced him to abdicate, his reign had been brought to an end in a wholly different way by the Senate. Talleyrand, vice-president of this body, who had for some time been intriguing in favor of the house of Bourbon, pronounced openly in favor of it before the sovereigns when they entered Paris. 'The regency,' he said, ' was an intrigue; the Bourbons alone were a principle.' He convoked the Senate on April 1st, and on April 2d it voted the deposition of Napoleon and his family. This decision was ratified the next day by the Corps Législatif.

Then occurred the abdication in favor of his family, which had the support of the army. The instrument was brought to Paris by not less than three famous marshals, Ney and Macdonald having been joined on their way from Fontainebleau by Marmont. The two solutions were thus brought at the same time before the allied sovereigns, of whom Alexander was not favorably disposed to the Bourbons, and Francis was the father of Marie Louise. For a moment the balance trembled.

But Marmont had been brought in contact, during his defence of Paris, with Talleyrand, and had committed himself to him before the marshals took their independent course. After evacuating Paris he had been stationed on the Essonne. Here he had entered into an engagement to place his corps at the service of the new provisional Government which the Senate had constituted; the arrangement was that on April 5th the corps should quit its position and march into Normandy. But when the marshals passing through his camp from Fontainebleau told him of their commission, he had revealed the secret of this engagement with expressions of penitence: he had countermanded his orders to the inferior officers, and had gone with the marshals to Paris. In his absence, however, General Souham, influenced by a fear that the plot had become known to Napoleon, gave orders to the troops to march on Versailles. This appearance of division in the army was fatal to Napoleon's family. It decided Alexander to declare for the Bourbons, and Caulaincourt was instructed to demand from Napoleon an abdication pure and simple. In return he was to retain the title of emperor, and to have the island of Elba in sovereignty, while Marie Louise was to have a principality in Italy. The unconditional abdication was signed at Fontainebleau on April 11.

By an irony of fortune the Government founded at Brumaire, in which everything had been sacrificed to military efficiency, was the only one of the three Governments of France since 1789 which actually succumbed before an invader. The total result of so many conquests was that France, which, when Napoleon's name was first heard of, was in substantial possession of Belgium, the left bank of the Rhine, Savoy, and Nice, had now lost the first two acquisitions; and we shall see what measures he took to deprive her of the other two. His fatal power of bewildering the popular mind was already at work again. This last campaign, the most unpatriotic he ever fought, had seemed to redeem his faults, and had given him the name of a heroic defender of his country. It was a view which made way fast, as soon as he had the restored Bourbons for a foil.

§ 4. *He retires to Elba. — Disquiet in France. — The Hundred Days. — Battle of Waterloo.*

In the mean time however all the hatred, long suppressed, of individuals and of parties broke loose upon him. For the moment he seems to have utterly lost heart. On the night of April 11, after signing the unconditional abdication, he is said to have taken a dose of a poison which ever since the Russian campaign he had kept by him. But vomitings, we are told, came on and saved him. On the 20th, when he bade farewell to his soldiers, he had resolved to live, in order 'to record the great deeds we have done together.' He soon found another object for life; but a year later, after another downfall far more complete and ignominious, he clings to life, and he clings to it afterwards in captivity. The soldiers idolized him still, and his parting scene at Fontainebleau, when he kissed the eagle, was pathetic; but when he reached the south of France, he met with other demonstrations of feeling. At Avignon and Orgon the crowd attacked the carriages, and wanted to throw the tyrant into the Rhone. He was compelled to disguise himself. At the coast he was met by an English frigate, which landed him on

May 4th at Porto Ferraio, in Elba. It seems to have been arranged among the sovereigns that his wife and child were not to rejoin him, nor did he complain of this. Marie Louise set out for her old home on April 23d, and was at Schönbrunn again before the end of May. About the same time Josephine died at Malmaison, in the arms of her children Eugène and Hortense.

It must have occurred to Napoleon very soon after his arrival in Elba that he was not yet driven to autobiography. Never was a great state in a position so untenable and monstrous as France after he quitted the helm. In twenty years of thrilling events, in the emotions first of tragedy and then of epic poetry, the French had forgotten the Bourbon court, when suddenly the old Comte de Provence (under the name of Louis XVIII) and the Comte d'Artois, Condé and the Duc d'Angoulême and the Orpheline du Temple, reappeared and took possession of the country, before even a royalist party had formed itself in France. Politically indeed they brought liberty, for they created a parliament, where all assemblies had been mute and servile for fourteen years; but they unsettled all domestic affairs, the position of public men, the prospects of the army, the title of estates, in a manner so sudden and intolerable,

especially at a moment when the country had
suffered conquest from without, that some new
convulsion seemed manifestly imminent. Disgraced, bewildered, and alarmed at the same time,
the French could think with regret even of the
reign of Napoleon. The wholesale massacre of
the last two years might have been expected to
seem like a bad dream as soon as the spell was
snapped, but it began to seem regrettable in comparison with the present humiliation. Another
event happened which was like a new revolution.
The prisoners and the troops shut up in German
fortresses returned to France under the treaty, perhaps not less than 300,000 men. What could be
more evident than that, if all these soldiers could
take the field again, and under Napoleon, France
might yet escape the humiliation of a Government
imposed by the foreigner, and perhaps also recover
her lost frontiers? The congress of Vienna entered upon business in September, and with this
a new chapter of politics opened. France ceased
to be the general bugbear, and new alliances began to be formed in order to check the aggressive
spirit of Russia. The European Coalition, once
dissolved, might prove not easy to reconstitute.
Internal politics also had altered. A wild party
of ultras had sprung up among the royalists; the

church was beginning to give disquiet to the holders of national property; the army was enraged by seeing *émigrés*, who had fought against France, appointed in great numbers to the command of regiments.

It was not the first time that Napoleon had gone into a sort of exile. As he had disappeared in the East, and returned to make Brumaire, so he might come from Elba to rescue France. The situation was not less intolerable than in 1799. As then, so now, had he not returned, a revolution would nevertheless have taken place. Fouché was weaving a military plot, which would have carried to power perhaps the Duke of Orleans, perhaps the King of Rome.

He entered upon the last of his thousand adventures on February 26, 1815, when he set sail from Porto Ferraio with Generals Bertrand and Drouot and 1,100 soldiers. On March 1st he reached the French coast at the gulf Jouan between Cannes and Antibes. Twenty days after he entered the Tuileries in triumph.

He had judged the feelings of the army correctly, and also the effect which would be produced by his prodigious fame. These causes were more than enough to overthrow a Government so totally without root as that of the Bourbons.

From the coast he took the way across the mountains of Provence by Sisteron and Gap to Grenoble. The soldiers sent from this town to stop him were disarmed when he uncovered his breast and asked, Which of them would fire on his emperor? He was then joined by the royalist La Bédoyère. Macdonald at Lyons stood firm, but was deserted by his soldiers. Ney, who commanded in the east, at first declared himself violently against his old chief, but the military feeling afterwards gained him, and he joined Napoleon at Auxerre. The king left the Tuileries on the 19th, retiring northward, and on the next day Napoleon entered Paris.

At Brumaire he had put down Jacobinism, and given the nation order and repose. Now he was summoned, in the name of independence, to protect the acquisitions of the Revolution, and to defend the national honor against the triumphant foreigner. The Hundred Days are the period of popular or democratic imperialism. Those who sided with him told him frankly that he must turn over a new leaf, and he professed himself ready to do so. It would be rash to say that this was impossible. He was but in his forty-sixth year; his return from Elba was an astonishing proof that he still possessed that elasticity of spirit, that power of grasping the future, which he had often shown so remarkably. Here then, as at a second Brumaire, might begin a third Napoleonic period. The mad crusade against England and the world-empire which sprang out of it were now to be forgotten; the oppressor of Tyrol and Spain was to stand out as a heroic representative of the free modern people against the Holy Alliance. This last and most audacious of his transformations was already most prosperously begun. But at this point fortune deserted him once for all. Napoleon Liberator remained a poetical idea, transforming his past life into legend, and endowing French politics with a new illusion; the attempt to realize it came to an end in a hundred days (March 13 to June 22).

The ultimate cause of this failure seems to have been a change in Napoleon himself. It had long been remarked that the Emperor Napoleon was wholly different from the General Bonaparte of the Italian campaigns. Bonaparte had been lean, shy, laconic, all fire and spirit, the very type of republican virtue imagined by Rousseau; the Emperor was fat and talkative, and had his fits, according to Marmont, of indolent ease. Once or twice there had been attacks of illness, by which he had been temporarily incapacitated; but this had been hushed up. On the whole he had never yet been wanting to himself. In the campaign of 1814 his activity had been prodigious, and the march to Paris in twenty days, with which he had opened 1815, had been a great display of vigor. But he could not maintain himself at this level. A physical decay had begun in him, affecting through his body, not indeed his mind, but his will and his power of application. 'I do not know him again,' said Carnot. 'He talks instead of acting, he the man of rapid decisions; he asks opinions, he the imperious dictator, who seemed insulted by advice; his mind wanders, though he used to have the power of attending to everything when and as he would; he is sleepy, and he used to be able to sleep and wake at pleasure.' This last symptom was the most striking; in some of the most critical and terrible moments of the Waterloo campaign he seems to have been scarcely able to keep himself awake.

The constitutional history of the Hundred Days may be despatched summarily, since it led to nothing. On March 13 an imperial decree was issued from Lyons dissolving the two chambers established by the Bourbons, and convoking an extraordinary assembly in Field of May for the purpose 'of correcting and modifying our constitutions, and of assisting at the coronation of the Empress, our dear and well-beloved spouse, and of our dear and well-beloved son.' But the prospect soon changed, and, as it was necessary that the empire, like the monarchy, should have its charter, it seemed impossible to wait till May. Napoleon had recourse to Benjamin Constant, that is, he marked his change of policy by sending for the leader of the opposition. The 'Acte Additionnel aux Constitutions de l'Empire,' dated April 22, was drawn by Constant, examined by a committee, and then adopted by the council of state. The most remarkable feature of it is the preamble, in which he explains his change of attitude by saying that 'formerly he had endeavored to organize a grand federal system in Europe, which he had regarded as agreeable to the spirit of the age and favorable to the progress of civilization,' that 'for this purpose he had adjourned the introduction of free institutions,' but that 'henceforward he had no other object but to increase the prosperity of France by strengthening public liberty.'

This neat misrepresentation deserves notice as having imposed on many people. For the rest it is to be observed that the act creates an hereditary peerage. The Field of May was held, but not till June 1. Napoleon appeared in a grand costume and distributed flags, but the 'well-beloved spouse and son' were not there; Europe had declared against him. On the 12th he set out for the campaign.

The Great Powers had issued, immediately on hearing of Napoleon's disembarkation (March 13th), a declaration putting him outside all civil and social relations, and consigning him to public vengeance as 'an enemy and disturber of the peace of the world.' On March 25th they reconstituted the Coalition. Was this a disappointment to Napoleon? A war of liberation was perhaps necessary to him. To be freely accepted by the French people, and then to be rejected by Europe, gave him precisely the opportunity he sought of standing forth as the heroic champion of national independence. He had now all the soldiers who at the time of his first fall had been locked up in fortresses or foreign prisons. His position was therefore such as it had been in 1813, not in 1814, and he proposed to defend not a vast empire but simply France, so that he had on his side patriotism and liberalism. All this, and his own genius! Would not so much suffice? Probably he remembered Brumaire, how low the fortune of France at that time had been, and how suddenly Marengo had restored all. For the moment, however, the inequality of numbers was great. In June the allies had in the field more than 700,000, Napoleon little more than 200,000, men. There were already English troops in Belgium, where they were engaged in establishing the new kingdom of the Netherlands, and there were Prussian troops in the Rhenish province which had just been given to Prussia. It was a question for Napoleon, whether he should assume a defensive attitude and allow the allies to invade France—this in itself would have suited his new policy best — or carry the war into Belgium, a country long united with France, and attack the English and Prussians. He shrank from inflicting a new invasion upon France, especially on account of the strength of the royalist party in many regions, and thus it was that the scene of the campaign was laid in Belgium. The English had their head-quarters at Brussels, the Prussians at Liège. He formed the plan of dividing them and beating them in turn, as he had served the Austrians and Sardinians at the very beginning of his career. Many circumstances, however, were different. Wellington and Blücher with Gneisenau were superior to Colli and Beaulieu; the Napoleon of 1815 was vastly inferior to the Bonaparte of 1796.

Of all the Napoleonic campaigns this proved by

far the most rapid and decisive. Even the Marengo campaign had lasted a month, but this was decided in three days. Leaving Paris on the 12th, Napoleon was in Paris again on the 21st, his own fate and that of his empire and that of France decided. Everything concurred to make this short struggle the most interesting military occurrence of modern history: its desperate intensity, its complete decisiveness, the presence for the first and last time of the English army in the front of the European contest, the presence of the three most renowned commanders, Napoleon, Wellington, and Blücher. Accordingly it has been debated with infinite curiosity, and misrepresented on all sides with infinite partiality. Napoleon's army amounted to 122,401 men; it contained a large number of veterans, besides many who had seen the campaigns of 1813-14, and was perhaps the finest army he had ever commanded. That of Wellington was composed of Englishmen, Hanoverians, Brunswickers, Nassauers, Germans, and Netherlanders; the total is stated at 105,950. But in the Netherlands of the newly established kingdom no confidence could be placed, and yet these amounted to nearly 30,000; the English too (about 35,000) were in great part raw recruits (the Peninsular veterans being mainly absent in

America): altogether Wellington pronounced it 'the worst army ever brought together.' The army of Blücher numbered 116,897 disciplined troops, animated by an intensely warlike spirit. Napoleon's opening was prosperous. He maintained so much secrecy, and used so much rapidity, that he succeeded in throwing himself between the two armies. On the 15th he advanced and occupied Charleroi. On the 16th he engaged the Prussians at Ligny and the English at Quatrebras, desiring to block the cross-road between Quatrebras and Sombreffe, and so to sever the two armies. Napoleon personally commanded against the Prussians, and here he gained his last victory. The battle was very bloody; about 12,000 Prussians fell, and Blücher himself was wounded. At Quatrebras Ney met Wellington, and was forced to retreat. But the defeat of Blücher made it necessary for Wellington to retire on Brussels in order to effect a junction with the Prussians. The 17th was spent in this retrograde movement, and on the 18th Wellington accepted battle on the heights of St. Jean, from which the French name the day, while the English give it the name of Waterloo, a village four miles nearer to Brussels, where Wellington wrote his despatch. He accepted battle in full reliance upon the help of the

Prussians, who are not therefore to be considered as having saved him from defeat.

Military writers point out several errors, some of them considerable, committed by Wellington, but their criticism of Napoleon, which begins by sweeping away a mass of falsehood devised by him and his admirers in order to throw the blame upon others, is so crushing that it seems to show us Napoleon, after his brilliant commencement, acting as an indolent and inefficient general. He first, through mere want of energy, allows the Prussians to escape him after Ligny, and then sends Marshal Grouchy with 33,000 men in the wrong direction in pursuit of them. Owing to this mismanagement, Grouchy is at Wavre on the day of the battle of Waterloo, fighting a useless battle against the Prussian corps of Thielemann, while Blücher is enabled to keep his engagement to Wellington. Everywhere during these days Napoleon appears negligent, inactive, inaccessible, and rather a Darius than an Alexander, so that it has been plausibly maintained that he must have been physically incapacitated by illness. The battle itself was one of the most remarkable and terrible ever fought, but it was perhaps on both sides rather a soldiers' than a general's battle. It consisted of five distinct attacks on the English position :— (1) an attack on the English right by the division Reille, (2) an attack on the left by the division D'Erlon (here Picton was killed), (3) a grand cavalry attack, where the splendid French cavalry 'foamed itself away' upon the English squares, (4) a successful attack by Ney on La Haye Sainte (which Wellington is thought to have too much neglected; it was after this that the French prospect seemed brightest), (5) the charge of the guard. In the middle of the third act of this drama the Prussians began to take part in the action. The battle seems to have begun about 11.30, and about 8 o'clock in the evening the cry 'Sauve qui peut' arose from the guard. A general advance of the English decided the victory, and then the pursuit was very thoroughly accomplished by the Prussians under Gneisenau. Napoleon at first took refuge in a square. At Genappe he left this, and arrived at Charleroi about daybreak with an escort of about twenty horsemen.

§ 5. *The second Abdication. — Surrender to England. — Exile in St. Helena. — Autobiography.*

He lost probably more than 30,000 out of 72,000 men, but the grand army was utterly dissolved. The whole loss of the allies was somewhat more than 22,000. Had Napoleon been victorious, he would but have opened the war prosperously, for half a million soldiers, in addition to those of Wellington and Blücher, were on the march for France; being completely defeated, he had no resource, but was ruined at once. France was conquered, as she had been conquered the year before; but her second fall appears far more humiliating and dismal than her first, when we consider how enthusiastically she had rallied to Napoleon, and how instantaneously Napoleon and she had been struck down together. It was a moment of unrelieved despair for the public men who gathered round him on his return to Paris, and among these were several whose fame was of earlier date than his own. La Fayette, the man of 1789; Carnot, organizer of victory to the Convention; Lucien, who had decided the revolution of Brumaire,— all these met in that comfortless deliberation. Carnot was for a dictatorship of public safety, that is, for renewing his great days of 1793; Lucien too liked the Roman sound of the word dictator. 'Dare!' he said to his brother, but the spring of that terrible will was broken at last. 'I have dared too much already,' said Napoleon. Meanwhile, in the Chamber of Representatives the word was not dictatorship but liberty. Here La

Fayette caused the assembly to vote itself permanent, and to declare guilty of high treason whoever should attempt to dissolve it. He hinted that, if the word abdication were not soon pronounced on the other side, he would himself pronounce the word 'decheance.' The second abdication took place on June 22d. 'I offer myself a sacrifice to the hatred of the enemies of France. My public life is finished, and I proclaim my son, under the title of Napoleon II., Emperor of the French.' On the 25th he retired to Malmaison, where Josephine had died the year before. He had by no means yet ceased to hope. When his son was passed over by the Chamber of Representatives, who named an executive commission of five, he protested that he had not intended to make way for a new Directory; and, as Carnot and Caulaincourt were on this commission, the circumstances of Brumaire seem to have flashed into his memory. He saw again two Directors supporting him, and the other three (Fouché, Grenier, and Quinette—'a traitor and two babies,' as he expressed it) might remind him of Barras, Moulins, and Gohier. On the 27th he went so far as to offer his services once more as general, 'regarding myself still as the first soldier of the nation.' He was met by a refusal, and left Malmaison on the 29th for Rochefort, well furnished with books on the United States.

France was by this time entering upon another Reign of Terror. Massacre had begun at Marseilles as early as the 25th. What should Napoleon do? He had been formerly the enemy of every other nation, and now he was the worst enemy, if not of France, yet of the triumphant faction in France. He lingered some days at Rochefort, where he had arrived on July 3d, and then, finding it impossible to escape the vigilance of the English cruisers, went on the 15th on board the 'Bellerophon' and surrendered himself to Captain Maitland. It was explained to him that no conditions could be accepted, but that he would be 'conveyed to England to be received in such manner as the Prince Regent should deem expedient.' He had written at the Île d'Aix the following characteristic letter to the Prince Regent:—'Royal Highness,—A prey to the factions which divide my country and to the enmity of the powers of Europe, I have terminated my public career, and I come, like Themistocles, to seat myself at the hearth of the British people. I place myself under the protection of its laws, which I claim from your Royal Highness as the most powerful, the most constant, and the most generous of my enemies.'

It was perhaps the only course open to him. In France his life could scarcely have been spared, and Blücher talked of executing him on the spot where the Duc d'Enghien had fallen. He therefore could do nothing but what he did. His reference to Themistocles shows that he was conscious of being the worst enemy that England had ever had. Perhaps he remembered that at the rupture of the treaty of Amiens he had studied to envenom the contest by detaining the English residents in France. Still he might reflect, on the other hand, that England was the only great country which had not been trampled down and covered with massacre by his soldiers. It would have been inexcusable if the English Government had given way to vindictive feelings, especially as they could well afford to be magnanimous, having just won the greatest of all victories. But it was necessary to deprive him of the power of exciting new wars, and the experiment of Elba had shown that this involved depriving him of his liberty. The frenzy which had cost the lives of millions must be checked. This was the principle laid down in the declaration of March 15th, by which he had been excommunicated as a public enemy. It was therefore necessary to impose some restraint upon him. He must be separated from his party and from all the revolutionary party in Europe. So long as he remained in Europe this would involve positive imprisonment. The only arrangement therefore which would allow him tolerable personal comfort and enjoyment of life, was to send him out of Europe. From these considerations grew the decision of the Government to send him to St. Helena. An Act of Parliament was passed 'for the better detaining in custody Napoleon Bonaparte,' and another Act for subjecting St. Helena to a special system of government.

He was kept on board the 'Bellerophon' till August 4th, when he was transferred to the 'Northumberland.' On October 15th he arrived at St. Helena, accompanied by Counts Montholon, Las Cases, and Bertrand, with their families, General Gourgaud, and a number of servants. In April, 1816, arrived Sir Hudson Lowe, an officer who had been knighted for bringing the news of the capture of Paris in 1814, as governor.

The rest of his life, which continued till May 5, 1821, was occupied partly in quarrels with this governor, which have now lost their interest, partly in the task he had undertaken at the time of his first abdication, that of relating his past life. He did not himself write this narrative, nor does it appear that he even dictated it word for word.

It is a report made partly by General Gourgaud, partly by Count Montholon, of Napoleon's impassioned recitals; but they assure us that this report, as published, has been read and corrected throughout by him. It gives a tolerably complete account of the period between the siege of Toulon and the battle of Marengo. On the later period there is little, except a memoir on the campaign of 1815, to which the editors of the *Correspondence* have been able to add another on Elba and the Hundred Days.

These memoirs have often been compared to the *Commentaries* of Cæsar, and their value would indeed be priceless, if they related to a period imperfectly known. But an age which has abundance of information, and takes history very seriously, is struck particularly by the elaborate falsifications which they contain. A vast number of misstatements, many of them evidently intentional, have been brought home to him, and in several cases he has tried to foist into history apocryphal documents.

By dwelling almost exclusively upon the earlier period and on the Waterloo campaign, they helped forward the process by which he was idealized after his death. They reminded the world that the Prometheus now agonizing on the lonely rock, who had lately fallen in defending a free nation against a coalition of kings and emperors, was the same who, in his youth, had been the champion of the First French Republic against the First Coalition. They consigned the long interval to oblivion. Hence the Napoleonic legend, which has grown up in the very midst of the 19th century, and would perhaps never have been seriously shaken but for the failure of the Second Empire. Look at Napoleon's career between 1803 and 1814, when it was shaped most freely by his own will; you see a republic skilfully undermined and a new hereditary monarchy set up in its place. This new monarchy stands out as the great enemy and oppressor of nationalities, so that the nationality movement, when it begins in Spain and Tyrol and spreads through North Germany, is a reaction against Napoleon's tyranny. But in 1815 he succeeded in posing as a champion and martyr of the nationality principle against the Holy Alliance. The curtain fell upon this pose. It brought back the memory of that Bonaparte, who at the end of the 18th century had seemed the antique republican hero dreamed of by Rousseau, and men forgot once more how completely he had disappointed their expectations. By looking only at the beginning and at the end of his career, and by disregarding all the intermediate period, an imaginary Napoleon has been obtained, who is a republican, not a despot, a lover of liberty, not an authoritarian, a champion of the Revolution, not the destroyer of the Revolution, a hero of independence, not a conqueror, a friend of the people, not a contemner of the people, a man of heart and virtue, not a ruthless militarist, cynic, and Machiavellian. This illusion led to the restoration of the Napoleonic dynasty in 1852.

He died of an ulcer in the stomach on May 5, 1821. In his will he declared himself a Catholic, wished his ashes to repose 'on the banks of the Seine, in the midst of the French people whom he had loved so well,' spoke tenderly of Marie Louise and his son, and of all his relatives except Louis, whom he 'pardoned' for the libel he published in 1820, disavowed the *Manuscrit de Sainte Hélène*, a mystification which had recently had much success, defended the execution of D'Enghien, imputed the two conquests of France to Marmont, Augereau, Talleyrand, and La Fayette, whom he 'forgave,' and devoted the English oligarchy, to whom he ascribed his premature death, to the vengeance of the English people. In a codicil he added a truly Corsican touch, bequeathing 10,000 francs to the subaltern officer Cantillon, 'who has undergone a trial upon the charge of having endeavored to assassinate Lord Wellington, of which he was pronounced innocent. Cantillon had as much right to assassinate that oligarchist as the latter had to send me to perish upon the rock of St. Helena.'

He was buried at Longwood in St. Helena; but in the reign of Louis Philippe his remains were removed by permission of the English Government to the Invalides at Paris, where a stately dome was erected over the sarcophagus that contains them.

NAPOLEON'S PLACE IN HISTORY.

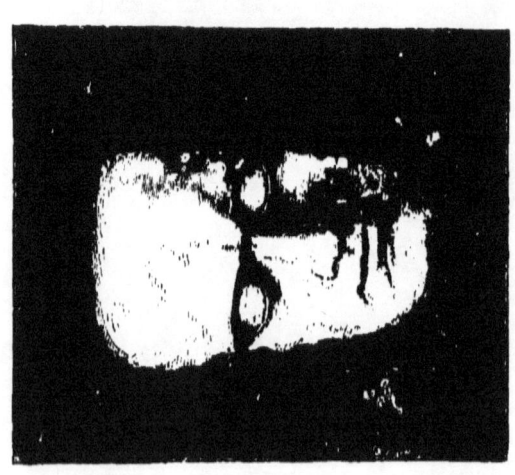

FROM A CAST OF THE FACE OF NAPOLEON, TAKEN AFTER DEATH.

NAPOLEON'S PLACE IN HISTORY.

AFTER reviewing the career of an historical person, we desire to form an estimate of his character and abilities. But to find a measure for great men, that is, men whose energy of action and whose sphere of action have been exceptional, is much more difficult than is usually supposed; and how extremely difficult it is in the case of Napoleon may be judged from the wide divergence in the estimates, whether of historians, such as Thiers on the one side and Lanfrey on the other, or of intelligent and impartial contemporaries, such as Goethe or Hazlitt on the one hand and Jefferson or Southey on the other; it may be judged, too, from the fact that no clear verdict of posterity has yet been, or seems about to be, pronounced upon him. He lends himself readily to unmeasured panegyric or invective, but scarcely any historical person is so difficult to measure. It would not be in accordance with the modest plan of this volume to offer a formal estimate, but an essay towards such an estimate, or in other words some suggestions as to the way in which such an estimate should be formed, may be acceptable.

The series of Napoleon's successes is absolutely the most marvellous in history. No one can question that he leaves far behind him the Turennes, Marlboroughs, and Fredericks; but when we bring up for comparison an Alexander, a Hannibal, a Cæsar, a Charles, we find in the single point of marvellousness Napoleon surpassing them all. Every one of those heroes was born to a position of exceptional advantage. Two of them inherited thrones; Hannibal inherited a position royal in all but the name; Cæsar inherited an eminent position in a great empire. But Napoleon, who rose as high as any of them, began life as an obscure provincial, almost as a man without a country. It is this marvellousness which paralyzes our judgment. We seem to see at once a genius beyond all estimate, a unique character, and a fortune utterly unaccountable.

There can, indeed, be no question that the personality and the fortune were both alike surprising. But it is only the combination of both which is altogether overwhelming. The first step towards a calm judgment is to separate the factors. I propose then to inquire how much and in what manner Napoleon was favored and shaped by circumstances, and afterwards to consider how much remains to be explained by personal idiosyncrasy.

CHAPTER I.

HOW FAR NAPOLEON WAS FAVORED BY CIRCUMSTANCES.

§ 1. *His Rise to Power.*

THERE are times, and these are the most usual, when the most wonderful abilities would not have availed to raise any man from such a station as that in which Napoleon was born to the head of affairs. But the last years of the eighteenth century formed an exceptional period, in which such an ascent was not only possible in France, but — and this is carefully to be marked — was quite possible without very extraordinary abilities. That particular part of Napoleon's career to which the Alexanders and Hannibals can show nothing parallel is, in fact, just the part which, in that exceptional time, was within the reach of an ordinary man.

The Revolution had broken the fixed mould in which European history had run for a thousand years, and had introduced a different sort of government, strange in the feudal world, but well known both to antiquity and to mediæval Italy, and not difficult to comprehend — Imperialism. It is a form which appears almost invariably when the growth of a great army coincides with the downfall of an ancient government. For this reason it had appeared in England, when a standing army had for the first time sprung up at the moment of the humiliation of the Stuart monarchy. For this reason it appeared now in France, when at the moment of the fall of the Bourbons the nation found itself plunged into an unprecedented war. Nothing short of a firmly established government can hold a great army in check; where that is wanting, the army assumes the place of government at once and without resistance, and this is Imperialism. Its first form is usually republican, a clique of officers exerting a secret control over the Supreme Assembly. Such was the system between 1648 and 1653 in the Long Parliament, such at Rome in the ten years of the Triumvirate, and such in France under the Directory, especially in the years between Fructidor and Brumaire. But in all these cases alike, the system speedily became monarchical. Cæsar pushed on one side alike the Senate and Pompey, Cromwell the Long Parliament, and Fairfax, and finally Bonaparte dismissed first the Directory, and then Moreau. When this change takes place the monarch created is always a successful general, and it is under this system that the fortunate adventurer is most frequently seen. The rise of Bonaparte was not very much more surprising than that of Cromwell, and in the classical age of Imperialism under the Roman Emperors it repeatedly happened that a rude soldier found himself master of the world, as in fact the real founder of Imperialism, Marius, had done.

Thus the miracle of Bonaparte's rise to power lies not so much in his personality as in the time. The tradition of a thousand years had been deserted, and what during that time had been unheard of was now possible and natural. We have seen that before Bonaparte returned from Egypt, other generals had been sounded with a view to a change in the Constitution. Had he been detained a little longer on the other side of the Mediterranean, or had he been captured by an English cruiser, we can scarcely conceive but that a revolution like that of Brumaire would nevertheless have taken place, and that it would have elevated some other adventurer to supreme power. Some officer of considerable military ability, but otherwise not extraordinary, would then have stood forth as the most powerful man in Europe.

Even if he failed, he too would have appeared to have a marvellous fortune. Perhaps a series of such adventurers would have arisen, like that of the American Presidents. Assuredly none would have taken a position like that of Napoleon, but a Moreau or a Bernadotte might have reigned with success and have won great victories. It is even most probable that not one would have failed so disastrously as Napoleon did in the end, and that Belgium and Savoy and the left bank of the Rhine would not have been lost again to France.

§ 2. *His Ascendency in Europe.*

When it is said that Bonaparte by his genius gave France an ascendency in Europe, the chronological succession of events is neglected, and far too much is attributed to Bonaparte, far too little to those who came before him. The war had raged for four years when Bonaparte began to command armies. Without the help of Bonaparte France had defeated and dissolved the Coalition, without his help she had become an ascendant Power, had conquered and parcelled out in departments Belgium, Savoy, and Nice, had occupied the whole left bank of the Rhine, and had reduced Holland to complete dependence. It was in this time also, and without the help of Bonaparte, that an unparalleled military power had grown up in France, that a new military system had been devised, and a new period of military glory introduced. This wonderful revolution had been made before he appeared; the military power was already becoming supreme, the age of conquest was already begun when he first became prominent. Jourdan, Pichegru, Moreau, Carnot, not Bonaparte, directed the change. During the next four years the process continued without interruption; Fructidor (1797) may be said to have definitively established the military government; Lombardy, Central Italy, Switzerland, and the left bank of the Rhine were added to the practical conquests of France, and the Germanic system received a fatal blow. This, too, happened before Bonaparte rose to the head of affairs; he had indeed a share, and the greatest share, in these changes; but much was still done without him; he did not give the impetus, but followed an impulse which had been given by others; had he never appeared, the character of government in France, and the position of France in Europe, would have been substantially the same. Even after Brumaire, it is to be remarked that the victory which decided the war and gave peace to the Continent was not won by Bonaparte but by Moreau.

In his first years, then, Bonaparte is borne on a mighty tide. During this period we can see plainly that his career is only unprecedented, because an unprecedented convulsion had introduced it. Revolutionary times afford the occasion of exceptional careers, and if Napoleon's career was not only exceptional but absolutely unique, it was because the French Revolution also was unique.

§ 3. *His Conquests.*

A similar remark is to be made upon the unparalleled series of triumphant campaigns which followed his assumption of supreme power. The Revolution had created a vast machinery both of military and political power, which now fell readymade into his hands. In his position, the same amount of energy would produce vastly greater results than it could produce in the hands of Frederick or Marlborough. The genius of a leader is to be measured not so much by the actual results achieved as by the difficulties overcome. When we follow William III. in his contest with Louis XIV., Frederick in the Seven Years' War, Washington in the American War, and Wellington in the Peninsula, we remark how they were overmatched, how insufficient were the means at their disposal, and then how they supplied all deficiencies from the resources of their own genius. The case of Bonaparte after Brumaire is opposite to these. Never have means so vast, nor such absolute control over those means, been granted to any modern ruler.

Look first at the means. France had in seven years of war gained a position of prodigious military advantage, and controlled the Continent as no Power had done before. Moreover, in these years she had formed the habit and the taste for war on a large scale. The nation had adapted itself through necessity to the practice of putting vast armies into the field; the soldiers were inspired with heroism through the belief, which at the outset had been well grounded, that they were devoting themselves to their country, and through the belief, which was not entirely groundless, that they were the champions of great principles. By seven years of effort and hardship their valor had been tempered, they had acquired discipline. We may search history in vain for another military instrument of such efficiency and potency as this French army.

Remark next how unreservedly this instrument was now put at the service of Bonaparte. In most states war is felt as a burden, and borne with pain and reluctance; it involves taxation, which oppresses the population; it meets with opposition in assemblies and parliaments. In most states the skilled general is in the position of a servant, and has to render account either to a jealous sovereign or to a suffering and impatient community. Remember only how William was thwarted, how Marlborough was watched, calumniated, and at last overthrown, by the Opposition. As much as Napoleon's armies exceeded in number and efficiency those of Marlborough, so much was his authority greater, more easily and safely wielded. A number of causes had worked together for a long time to create in France an unlimited military authority. It was a country in which for a century and a half government had been despotic, and for a century great military enterprises had been undertaken, and had been unboundedly popular so long as they were successful. In the Revolution despotism had only taken a new shape, and it had become more energetic than under the Bourbons. It had been since 1793 the despotism of a military dictatorship, justified at the outset by the pressing military needs of a country invaded by a coalition, and pressing especially upon the army, where Houchard, Custine, and Beauharnais, had fallen by the guillotine. Just before Brumaire, the urgent need of 1793 had reappeared, for after a long course of victory the Republic had suffered reverses, and in 1799 France had been a second time threatened with invasion. The iron sceptre thus forged in the revolutionary fire now fell into the hand of Bonaparte, and for a long time all Frenchmen were glad to see it in such hands, for they could believe him to be more capable than Carnot, while he abjured, at the moment that he took it into his hand, all the excesses of Jacobinism. Meanwhile, parliaments had been discredited in France by ten years of failure. After they had been decimated and purged in as many revolutions as there were months in the revolutionary calendar, the time was come when Frenchmen desired to hear no more of them. Their debates were now no longer reported, and hence it was that at the moment when the mightiest and most disciplined army was put absolutely into the hands of the greatest military specialist, who was at the same time head of the State, the constitutional assemblies, which might have criticised his plans of war or checked his war budgets, were practically silenced.

The result is that, whereas other great generals have exhibited what great things can be done by small means, the career of Bonaparte after the beginning of his reign shows, on the other hand, the utmost extent of the performance possible to genius provided with unlimited means and facilities. This remark does not fully apply to his earlier campaigns, including that of Marengo; nor, again, does it apply to the defensive campaign of 1814; but it applies to the whole unparalleled series of triumphs that began with Ulm and ended with Dresden.

§ 4. *Was he Invincible?*

It has been frequently repeated that only in four of such a long and crowded series of battles was he defeated — that is, at Eylau, Aspern, Leipzig, and Waterloo; and it is added that of these defeats the first two were doubtful, that at Leipzig he was but 'pressed to the ground by thronging millions,' and that at Waterloo the fault lay with Grouchy, who mistook his orders. By representations such as these an impression is produced that in war at least his genius was unerring and unlimited, that it could even control fortune, and that it could but just barely be frustrated by the mistake of a subaltern, or by the sheer impossibility of the undertaking.

This is an illusion produced by the popular habit of regarding a war as consisting simply of a series of pitched battles and each battle as a sort of duel between the two commanders. The best military judges do indeed regard Napoleon as one of the greatest of tacticians, and as possessing in the highest degree the *coup d'œil*, promptitude, presence of mind, by which battles are won. But when in a very long series of battles a commander meets with scarcely any defeats, the most obvious inference surely is that he had very good and highly disciplined troops. In many of his campaigns, especially those of Marengo and of Austerlitz, the admirable efficiency of the army formed in the Revolution can be clearly discerned. Bonaparte reaped the benefit of the period of war which preceded his advent, and this benefit he enjoyed till he threw away in Russia that incomparable army. But a war consists of much more than battles, and indeed we should very much underrate Napoleon's own military genius if we regarded him simply as a winner of battles. Compared with other generals, he shows his superiority less in tactics than in strategy and in the comprehensive war-statesmanship by which a campaign on a large scale is planned. But if the highest genius may be displayed in strategy, the greatest mistakes may also be made in this department. It follows that a commander may suffer defeat, and that on the greatest scale, without personally losing battles; nay, that he may win all the battles of a campaign and yet lose the campaign itself.

We have only to apply this principle to Napoleon, and the illusion of his invincibility will disappear. We see in him a greater strategist than any that had appeared before him, but a strategist capable of great errors and failures. He achieves the most striking successes, but he also suffers the most complete and disastrous defeats, and his defeats are not less numerous than his successes. The most unfortunate general that ever lived, a Xerxes, a Darius, or Napoleon's own nephew, never underwent such a succession of crushing disasters as Napoleon in the years 1812, 1813, 1814, 1815. And if we look more closely we shall see that these were not his only failures, but that he suffered others scarcely less complete in earlier life, which, however, are little remarked, because he succeeded in covering the memory of them in a blaze of glory. The glory of Austerlitz, for example, covers the total failure of his plans for the invasion of England, plans devised by himself, and the failure of which ought to lower our opinion of his good fortune as much as the success of them would have heightened it — plans which ended in the absolute ruin of the French naval power. In like manner the successful *coup d'tat* of Brumaire and the splendid opening of the Consulate conceal from our view the failure of the Egyptian expedition. Yet what failure could be more unrelieved and disastrous? It ended simply in the re-establishment of English supremacy in the Mediterranean, from which sea the English fleets had been withdrawn, and in the acquisition of Malta by England. Yet this was Napoleon's favorite enterprise, impressed more than most others with the mark of his peculiar genius. Moreover, when we inquire into the cause of the failure we discover not some impediment that could not reasonably be anticipated, but an ordinary miscalculation vitiating the whole design — namely, an extravagant under-estimate of the naval power of England.

All these considerations taken together show that Napoleon's career, though the most extraordinary on record, does not differ in kind from other great careers, but only in degree; that we need not regard it superstitiously, as though either fate were specially interested in it, or something more than mere genius, some supernatural valor and wisdom, were displayed in it. The explanation of the enormous scale of magnitude which prevails in this career is to be found in the French Revolution and in the turn which it had taken.

Influence of the Revolution. 253

An unprecedented convulsion made the waves run high, and it so happened that all the wild forces and passions let loose in the Revolution had converted themselves into military force. An unparalleled army was created, and was then handed over, along with the government of a great European state, into the hands of a consummate military specialist and a most energetic character. He wielded this weapon with absolute control, and the result was a series of gigantic military enterprises, conducted always ably, but for the most part also recklessly, and resulting in some prodigious triumphs, and then in a series of still more prodigious disasters.

CHAPTER II.

HOW FAR NAPOLEON WAS SHAPED BY CIRCUMSTANCES.

§ 1. *His Lawlessness.*

In the quality, as well as in the quantity, of his performance we may trace the working of circumstances. By circumstances he was shaped as well as favored.

In general, it is easy to over-estimate the importance of personality, the part which is played in human affairs by free-will. Those who have taken the most favorable, and those who have taken the most unfavorable view of Napoleon's character, seem alike to ascribe to that character a greater share in the events than it really had or could have. That he was scarcely governed at all by ordinary moral considerations, lies on the surface of his career, and those who try to defend his actions on accepted moral principles claim more for him than he ever claimed for himself, for he frequently repeated that morality was not intended for the class of men to which he belonged. Was he then above morality or below it? That is, was he a great genius in morals as in military science, flinging aside conventions only in order to be more faithful to great principles, doing more good, and accomplishing more for mankind by his audacious acts, apparently so lawless, than a timid morality could accomplish in ten times as many years? Or was he, on the other hand, a kind of incarnation of evil, a Satan such as Milton describes, solitary in the universe? Both views seem to attribute to him too much originality. He was a great soldier and a most powerful ruler, — that is, he had a great genius for action, but it is an error to attribute to him either the virtues or the vices of a philosopher. He neither had nor valued original ideas, but was a *virtuoso* in the art of availing himself of the new ideas which he found current. Especially when we consider his crimes and lawless acts, it becomes gradually clear that in his public morality Napoleon represents a peculiar demoralization, which had been gaining ground in Europe through the whole of the eighteenth century.

The partition of Poland is cited as one of the greatest of international crimes, and it may fairly be said that Napoleon's whole career consists of a series of such crimes. From the partition of Venice and the invasion of Turkey at the beginning of it, to the seizure of Spain, the spoliation of Prussia, and the invasion of Russia at a later time, we trace throughout the same lawless determination to make the utmost use of a military force such as had never been seen before and was not likely soon to appear again. Unrestrained spoliation is the rule, and it is cloaked with the most transparent pretexts. But the very name of the partition of Poland ought to warn us against regarding Napoleon as an inventor or originator of international lawlessness. The example had been given when he was a child. Nor was that example by any means isolated, nor was he the first to follow it. This is sufficiently shown by the fact that the second and third partitions of Poland, as well as the first, took place before the appearance of Napoleon, or by the fact that there was as much lawless violence in the revolutionary war between 1792 and 1796 as in the years that followed Napoleon's first campaign.

Personality exerts a fascinating influence upon us. We perceive far more distinctly, as it were, the deeds we can attribute to a single notable person, than similar deeds of which the responsibility is divided among many persons, of whom some may be obscure and some quite unknown. The enormous character of Napoleon's deeds would not strike us so much if the same deeds had been done by a succession of ordinary French ministries during the same space of time. The best proof of this is that we so seldom remark how the same lawless principles had been gathering head for a very long time in Europe, how many similar acts had been done before in the eighteenth century, how slight is the difference in moral principle, however great the difference in power and opportunity, between Napoleon and other rulers of that age. When we attend to this general character of the age, we come to see that the Napoleonic wars are only the fatal catastrophe towards which Europe had long been madly hurrying, the last paroxysm of the possessed before the evil spirit, which was the spirit of international cynicism, went out of him. We talk of the partition of Poland, but that deed was really not so exceptional, nor should we speak of it as the cause of the demoralization of Europe, but rather as one among several proofs that Europe was already demoralized.

Professor Stubbs has remarked that in the Middle Ages wars were waged for rights, but in modern times for interests. Till near the end of the seventeenth century, or as long as religion continued to be a leading international influence, it may be said that though there was much disorder and crime, sheer naked cynicism did not yet prevail in the intercourse of nations. But from the war of the Spanish Succession throughout the eighteenth century it may be said that, though there was some improvement in the manner in which war was conducted, it was undertaken on more unblushingly immoral grounds than either before or since. The old European system founded on the unity of religion had passed away, and the later system, founded on the struggle of two rival religions, had almost passed away too. On the other hand, the modern system, founded on nationality, only began to show itself at the French Revolution. Hence, whereas our nineteenth century wars are inspired by national patriotism, and the wars of the seventeenth century, even those of Louis XIV., have at least some, if only superficial, varnish of religion, those of the intermediate period — I speak of the Continental wars — are scarcely colored by any kind of moral pretext. It is the iron age of international relations, the age in which wars are waged simply to round off a territory, to give compactness to a state. The ominous word Partition, pronounced a little earlier in reference to the Spanish Empire, when it was hoped to accomplish by treaty between William III. and Louis XIV. the settlement which afterwards cost Europe a war, seems to govern the whole century. It would appear that the precedent set in the case of the Spanish Empire demoralized all the politicians of Europe. They saw on the one hand the Bourbon family gain a kingdom in spite of a solemn renunciation; on the other hand, a rearrangement of the map of Europe accomplished by force of arms. Henceforward every great royal demise became the signal for a war on the model of that of the Spanish Succession. Had Louis XV. died in childhood, as was expected, there would certainly have been in the twenties a war of the French Succession; there was a war of the Polish Succession in the thirties, and a war of the Austrian Succession in the forties, which last led to a second terrible struggle in the fifties; the seventies witnessed a partition of Poland, and a war of the Bavarian Succession; a partition of Turkey was attempted in the eighties. In the course of these wars kings and ministers accustomed themselves to contemplate rearrangements as large as those made at Utrecht, and to break engagements as sacred as that which had been broken by Louis XIV. This was seen in the eager haste with which so many sovereigns set aside the treaties in which they had pledged themselves to the Pragmatic Sanction. The spectacle then presented by Europe ought to show us that no partition of Poland, occurring thirty years later, was needed to demoralize statesmen.

It is easy to show that the French Revolution and Napoleon proceeded upon lines laid down in the former age. Their partitions and annexations were scarcely ever of their own imagining ; for the most part they did but take up schemes which had long been discussed, and had been attempted by other Governments. If they annexed Belgium, and gave Austria an indemnity in Italy, what was this but a modification of the grand scheme of Joseph II., which had so long occupied Europe, the scheme of exchanging Belgium against Bavaria ? It is to be observed that the same Joseph II. had also contemplated the acquisition of Venice. The partition of Poland is of course frequently referred to by the French diplomatists of the time as justifying, and even necessitating, a proportional aggrandizement of France ; and in like manner the Egyptian expedition was certainly undertaken by the French Government in emulation of the acts by which Russia and England had aggrandized themselves in the Oriental World.

The peculiar nature of this demoralization is best seen in the career of the Emperor Joseph II. It was Frederick who avowed it with the most cynical frankness, but for this very reason Frederick strikes us rather as personally an unprincipled man than as reflecting a special obliquity of the age. But of all sovereigns of modern Austria, Joseph appears as the most devoted to the public good, the most energetic reformer, the most indefatigable enemy of abuses; and yet this Emperor's foreign policy turns almost exclusively on partitions and lawless annexations, so that, had he been as successful as Napoleon, he would have been chargeable with almost as many international crimes. In general it may be remarked that in this period the sovereigns who are most enlightened and energetic, and open their minds most freely to the culture of the age, those to whom Continental Liberalism now looks back as to its founders, are specially lawless in acts of partition. The three great Liberal politicians of their time, Frederick, Joseph, and Catherine, combined to execute the partition of Poland. It is therefore the less surprising that when all the enlightenment of the age came to a head in the French Revolution, the principle of partition should have smuggled itself in with the principles of 1789, and that Bonaparte later, piquing himself upon being the successor of Frederick the Great in Europe, should have emulated not only Frederick's code, not only his vigorous domestic administration, but also the seizure of Silesia and the partition of Poland.

In international lawlessness, then, Bonaparte is not to be regarded as original. He is not precisely on this point to be considered more unprincipled than the other leading politicians. He can be charged only with going beyond them all in the ruthless energy with which he put the fashionable principle in practice, with committing crimes of the same kind, but in far greater number.

In short, it was inevitable, if the maxims preached in the earlier half of the century by Belleisle and Frederick, and enthusiastically adopted thirty years later by Joseph and Catherine, should come to be generally adopted, as at the time of the French Revolution they actually were, and if in the course of time some one European state should acquire a great military superiority to the others, that the consequence should be a sort of unlimited application of the principle of partition. This took place, and the result was the universal empire of Napoleon.

While his lawlessness in foreign policy is to be explained in this way, the violent acts he occasionally committed at home, the murder of D'Enghien and Palm, and some other deeds of violence, appear in like manner less original and unusual when they are taken in their place in French history. For if international politics had been demoralized gradually during the eighteenth century, the domestic politics of France had fallen into still wilder disorder through the Reign of Terror and the whole stormy course of the first republic. Deeds which, done in the name of a civilized government, shocked all Europe, were after all not so abnormal in the country which had so lately witnessed the storming of the Tuileries, the September massacres, the dictatorship and fall of Robespierre, and still more recently the cruel violence of Fructidor.

§ 2. *His Impressibility.*

Thus his lawlessness and violence are to be regarded less as inherent personal vices than as characteristics of the revolutionary age, which were borrowed by him. It is true that there was a certain original correspondence between his Corsican nature and the revolutionary way of thinking. Rousseau had introduced the fashion of primitive antique characters, and had actually pointed to Corsica as the home of such characters. There is evidence that in the early part of his career Bonaparte impressed the Parisian mind as realizing more genuinely than others the conception of Rousseau. His fierce energy and decision, his grave and stern demeanor, suited the age, as they would have seemed hopelessly incongruous in the time of Fleury or Bernis. But he owed far more to the suppleness, the ready knack of imitation and assimilation, which was concealed under that demeanor. He had a marvellous trick of adopting, parading, and profiting by, the ideas which prevailed around him. Hence he was a cynic in foreign policy, and at home a Terrorist under Robespierre, an Anti-Jacobin at Brumaire, and soon afterwards actually a Catholic. But it was in his Eastern campaign that he displayed most strikingly this turn for masquerading in strange intellectual costumes. In his fancy that the Deism of the French Revolution could be made to pass in the East for Mohammedanism he pushed it to an extreme, but in the reign of terror which he established in Egypt, and in the massacre at Jaffa, we recognize the same man, who could be a Frederick in Europe and a Jacobin or an Anti-Jacobin, as occasion might serve, at Paris. He has considered the manners of the East, assimilated them, and perceived that in Oriental war it is customary to massacre prisoners!

That he was in an eminent degree the child of circumstances, that while he appeared to control his age, he was in reality controlled and moulded by it, he acknowledged himself when he said of some one who had written upon his career, 'He speaks of me as if I were a person! I am not a person, I am a *thing*.'

It is involved in this that he can have been no more a prodigy of goodness than a prodigy of evil. The fancy that in his perpetual wars and rearrangements of the map of Europe he had in view some grand regeneration of humanity, perhaps some federation of Europe which should finally close the age of wars, has seldom been formally stated, but it has haunted many writers as at least partially or possibly true. What really actuated him will be discussed below, but he has no ideas peculiar to himself, only a talent for using and converting into force the ideas of his time.

§ 3. *His Relation to Parties.*

In this respect then he resembles a great party leader. But to what party did Napoleon belong? Was he a Liberal? Was he first a Liberal, and then a renegade? Or was he a Liberal who saw the necessity in an exceptional crisis of arming the Liberal cause with irresistible power, and so created a dictatorship in his own favor? Or was he no Liberal at all, but a reactionary, or even a tyrant and a mere selfish adventurer? I have myself laid little stress upon his hostility to liberty, nor have I been able to discover that, after having begun as an enthusiastic and glorious champion of freedom, he was gradually corrupted by power so as to become a tyrant. His rule was from the beginning despotic, and just as much so when he was called First Consul as when he was called Emperor. If he varied at all, it was only in dropping a few republican phrases, which had never been intended but as a blind for public opinion. But in despotism, too, he was not original. He invented nothing, but was the creature of circumstances. For before his advent, France had known since 1792 no other form of government but an extreme despotism. The Jacobinical party, which had been supreme in the main during the whole period, advocated a far stronger and severer form of government than had been known before even in the despotic states of Europe. It was this iron system that Bonaparte inherited; he made it more systematic, less violent, and much more endurable to the majority of the people. Assuredly he did not dream of abolishing it, and introducing in its place a system of liberty. But he destroyed no liberty, for there was none to destroy; and, indeed, if it may be asserted of certain nations in certain circumstances that they are unfit for liberty, perhaps this may be asserted of the French in 1800, demoralized as they were by eight years of the most furious internal discord. It has often been pointed out that the Revolution did not achieve, nor indeed seriously aim at, political liberty. As to the social liberties, the civil equality, which had been the fruit of the first Revolution (that of 1789), this was maintained on the whole by Napoleon. His system seemed on the whole a return to the first Revolution, and an abandonment of the second or Jacobinical Revolution (that of 1792). As compared with the old monarchies of Europe, Napoleonic France still seemed Liberal, and Napoleon himself ranked in Europe as a great Liberal ruler, as a successor of the Josephs and Catherines.

To some extent no doubt he abandoned even the principles of the first Revolution. He abandoned the civil constitution of the clergy, and restored by the Concordat the ancient connection of the Church in its ancient Papal form with the

State. It is to be remembered, however, that the Church so restored was a disendowed and humbled Church, from which the State might be thought to have little to fear. Again, at a later time he violated the principles of the Revolution by creating a nobility. But this was at a time when the conquest of Germany had modified the French State in its very foundations, and when the French Revolution itself seemed to have been superseded by a new or European revolution.

The second or Jacobinical Revolution he did indeed renounce wholly. But he did so at once and avowedly at the moment of assuming power, and in doing so he recanted little. Before that time he had not been properly a politician; that is, he had had no politics but foreign politics. It would be unreasonable to call him a renegade for now abandoning Jacobinism, on the ground that he had been a Jacobin at Vendémiaire, and had often talked Jacobinism since; in those days he had talked without responsibility, not as a politician but as a soldier.

§ 4. *His Significance in French History.*

Since, then, circumstances had so great a share in moulding Napoleon, how came they in this instance to mould a figure so colossal? In other words, what does he represent? Or is it possible that such a mighty display of power can be ascribed to no single and simple cause, but only to a multitude of secondary causes accidentally combined? In some sense surely he represents the spirit of the Revolution; and it is difficult not to think — however plainly the facts may seem to refute it — that that spirit was in some sense a spirit of liberty. Assuredly a new feeling of ardor, a new sense of health and power, had taken possession of the nation, and found expression, first, in the enthusiasm of the soldiers who conquered Belgium and the left bank of the Rhine before Napoleon's name was heard; and later, in the absorbing enthusiasm with which the hosts of France regarded *him*. But great confusion is produced by using the word 'liberty' to express any kind of enthusiasm which may inspire a community, even when that community remains under the yoke of an iron government. Some more precise and appropriate term is needed. It was not the personal idea of liberty, but rather a sense of the greatness of France that inspired those armies. The principles of '89 had, as it were, made all Frenchmen feel themselves citizens — that is, not so much free, as having an interest in the State. It is not in liberty that the subjects of the Convention or of Napoleon differ from the subjects of Louis XIV., but in the feeling that the Government, however absolute, was *their* Government. So distinct is this from liberty, that in the period when the feeling was fresh it gave a new energy to despotism. For the people took a pride in the strength and severity of the Government which was their own.

Not less great in the history of a people is the moment when it acquires this sense of membership in the State than the moment when it asserts its liberty; not less great, and wholly distinct. Then it ceases to regard Government with sullen dread as an enemy, or with resignation as an incomprehensible superior power, and begins to conceive it as a representative of itself, as the champion of its interests. In no civilized country had the superstitious view prevailed more absolutely than in the France of Louis XIV.; all the more inspiring was the change when now the rational view dawned upon the French mind, and the State appeared before their minds as a living organism. We may, perhaps, say that the effect of the Revolution was to make France not free, but *organic*. Parallel cases have occurred in our own age. Italy and Germany in like manner became organic by the abolition of petty, artificial, or foreign Governments, and by the establishment of a harmony between the State and the nation. In both cases the movement appeared to be at the moment rather unfavorable than favorable to the progress of liberty. In both cases the strongest form of government attainable was adopted.

Now it is instructive to observe that in both these cases, also, the earliest instinct of the State thus endowed with organic life was to extend its territory and make war upon its neighbors. The first step towards German unity was marked by an unsuccessful war for Schleswig-Holstein, the second step by a successful one, and the consummation of German unity was, as it were, attested by the conquest of Alsace and Lorraine. The kingdom of Italy could not be content without Rome and Venice, and still raises a wild cry of 'Italia Irredenta.'

In France the same instinct was at work when foreign war arose by a kind of necessity out of the Revolution. The speeches of Brissot de Warville, who inspired Dumouriez and prophesied of Napoleon, witness to the connection between the awakening sense of organic national life and the military ambition of revolutionary France. 'We are a hundred times as strong as we were,' he exclaims; 'now is the time to urge our ancient territorial claims.' Much has been said of the ambitious, unscrupulous character of the French nation; but in truth a false history had suggested to them unbounded pretensions, which no spirited nation, convinced of their justice, could renounce. They believed that they had a right to the frontiers of ancient Gaul, to the kingdom of Austrasia, which had been ruled by Charles the Great, and what not. Such illusions were in that age unavoidable, and they formed the basis of the foreign policy of the Revolution. Hence it is that as the German Revolution of our own age led directly to wars with Denmark, Austria, and France, so the French Revolution inevitably kindled war on the Rhine and in Belgium. But it is the notable peculiarity of the French Revolution that it was lost in the foreign wars which grew out of it. It alone therefore has its Napoleon.

This result was brought about in the following way: —

1. At the opening of the war France was invaded, threatened with dismemberment, and with a counter-revolution to be accomplished by force. This would at any time have called out a great movement of patriotism; at that moment of the new birth of the nation it kindled a patriotic ardor such as had never been witnessed before in one of

the large states of modern Europe. An immense national army sprang into existence, to which no army of earlier times was at all comparable. Insensibly from an army of patriotic defence this became an army of conquest, and a professional army from an army of citizens; but the old heroic spirit long survived the causes that had produced it, and the soldiers of Napoleon scarcely perceived till 1808 or 1809 (when Lannes in his dying moments reproached Napoleon with his ambition) that they had ceased to be patriots, and had become the tools of a conqueror.

2. The beginning of organic life in France was accompanied by the downfall of the ancient Government. In Italy and Germany, on the other hand, we have seen the King direct the movement and increase his power by means of it; and indeed had Louis XVI. been an energetic ruler, he might have acquired for himself much of the glory and power of Napoleon. But when the throne fell at the moment of the commencement of the war, the Revolution was drawn into another course, and this circumstance gave a new impulse to the warlike tendency. We have seen Germany put restraint upon herself, and deliberately pause in her career of victory. She has been able to do so because the military party has not been suffered to

become supreme. A contrary result was witnessed in France, because there, the Government having fallen, the military party itself was called upon to make a Government. Imperialism was established, and this is the form of government which, by the law of its nature, is most disposed to war, and conducts war most efficiently. We remember the brilliant foreign policy of Cromwell; the leader of French imperialism gave France a foreign policy as much more brilliant than Cromwell's as his army was greater and his authority more unquestioned.

3. The warlike policy gathered strength from success. It was itself in harmony with the tradition that had come down from Louis XIV. and Richelieu. It consoled the nation for the military humiliations of the last thirty years of Bourbon rule. And now Europe saw that the old barriers which had been set up at Utrecht against French aggression would not withstand for a moment the attack of the new national army. Now came to light the prodigious military advantage of an organic nation-state, with its inexhaustible supply of patriotic warriors, over inorganic artificial states such as those of Germany and Italy. Even in 1798, Napoleon himself being inactive or absent, France had a triumphant feeling of superiority to all Europe. Government after Government, Switz-

erland, the Papal State, Naples, went down before her reckless attacks, made almost in wantonness. And what gratified her ambitious instincts seemed justifiable to almost all French parties alike on one ground or other. To revolutionists conquest appeared as the diffusion of truth and liberty; to old-fashioned politicians it was a revival of the policy of Louis XIV., and an abandonment of the pernicious Austrian alliance; while theorists, if they followed an historical method, applauded the restoration of the empire of Charlemagne or of the ancient limits of Gaul; and if they reasoned *a priori*, and worshipped nature after the example of Rousseau, argued that a state founded on true natural principles should have natural frontiers.

This mighty spontaneous impulse of expansion, arising out of a fresh feeling of organic life in the French state, may on various grounds be blamed and criticised, but we can scarcely deny that it was great and poetical; we cannot but admire the generous ardor, the high energy and devotion to which it gave occasion; we cannot but admit that the series of wars which grew out of it is more agreeable to contemplate than the cynical struggles of princes for territory, which fill the annals of the former period. If, then, we find that Napoleon himself, after all criticism, remains a grand and

poetical figure, more interesting, more inspiring to
the imagination, than any mere successful general,
this is to be explained by the fact that he presided with an unparalleled authority and an unap-
proachable supremacy over this grand national
movement. But in stating this the words 'liberty' and 'liberalism' ought not to be used at all;
they belong to a different province. The greatness
and grandeur of Napoleon is in foreign or international politics; in domestic government he is
simply an emperor — that is, one who practises
the easy art of ruling a country through the army.

In the history of Europe it will be said of Napoleon as follows: that at the end of the eighteenth
century a movement began by which the great
Continental states, which till then had been inorganic, became conscious living organisms; that
this change took place in France first; that it gave
an extraordinary enlargement and sense of power to
the French mind; that, as it was at first peculiar
to France, it gave her an immense military advantage over other European states; that the perception
of this tempted her into great warlike enterprises;
that in these enterprises she found a leader of unrivalled energy, who conducted them with astonishing success — Napoleon. But it will also be
observed that this military advantage of France

was essentially temporary, and, as it were, accidental. Accordingly the immediate results of Napoleon's life have now all disappeared again. All that he gained for France she soon lost, and she has lost more since by attempting to continue his policy. In this respect Napoleon differs from the great historical personages to whom we may be disposed to compare him. The work of Alexander, Cæsar, Charles, even of Peter and Frederick, endured for centuries, so that they are remembered as founders and creators; but the work of Napoleon perished within his own lifetime, and the attempt to make him an object of veneration and imitation has failed ignominiously.

CHAPTER III.

WHAT NAPOLEON WAS IN HIMSELF.

IN inquiring how Napoleon was shaped by circumstances we considered how far he might have been carried by merely executing with military ability the ideas of others. Revolutionary France wanted a leader to perform for her one of the greatest of military tasks. Napoleon rose to the height of power because he presented himself as incomparably well qualified for the purpose.

But what was he in himself? That is, what were his own ideas and views?

Brumaire divides two very different periods in his life, which we might distinguish as the Bonaparte period and the Napoleon period. In the first he is a general, a servant of the state; in the second he is sovereign and master of the state. Now it is necessarily in the latter period that his personality is most important, because as a sovereign he shaped his own policy, and planned his own achievements; whereas, so long as he was a mere general, the principal responsibility lay with the

Directory. Even then, no doubt, he acted with much more freedom than an ordinary general in ordinary times. But though he was no mere executive agent in the partition of the Venetian Empire or in the Egyptian expedition, at least he did not make the war with Austria which caused the fall of Venice, nor the war with England which occasioned the Egyptian expedition. But after Brumaire, or at least after the treaties of Lunéville and Amiens, whatever is done by France is the act of Napoleon, and of him alone. What France does he does, and what he does he also designs and conceives in his own mind.

It follows that in this second period we have the best chance of discovering what he was in himself.

§ 1. *What was his Plan?*

We can scarcely be content with the current opinion that, no sooner had he become master of France than, yielding to his military instincts, he plunged into wars of conquest.

The simple fact is, that before Bonaparte began to reign there had been uninterrupted war with England since 1793, and war scarcely interrupted on the Continent since 1792, whereas after he began to reign, and had had time to make peace, the Continent was quiet for more than four years, and even the interminable rivalry of France and England ceased for a year. Even after the period of unbounded conquest had begun in 1805, Napoleon was not quite so continually at war as the number of his battles and victories might lead us to suppose. He did not take the field either in 1810 or 1811, and during those years there was peace on the Continent except in the Peninsula.

He was, in fact, not at all more aggressive than the Fructidorian republic, and for a long time he was decidedly less aggressive. During the Consulate he was renowned as the great peacemaker, as the friend of civilization, who alone had been found capable of healing the discord created by Jacobinism.

Are we then to suppose simply that the love of war mastered him by degrees; that after gratifying for a year or two the anti-Jacobinical party which had called him to the throne, he gave way again to his martial instincts; that after deliberately reckoning up his resources, and comparing them with those of Europe, he became convinced that he could found a universal empire, and proceeded to execute this design by breaking the peace of Amiens in 1803 ? Certainly his behavior, his diplomacy in 1803 and 1804 is that of a ruler intoxicated with the sense of overwhelming power, and eagerly desirous of war. But yet the theory that he formed at this time a conscious design of subjugating Europe seems far too simple to meet the facts. On that supposition he would hardly have proceeded as he did.

Any one who considers as a whole the history of Napoleon's empire will be struck by a strange peculiarity, which, if we regarded the empire as founded by deliberate design, would convict Napoleon of an unaccountable and fatal blunder. It was evidently his interest, first, not to engage England and the Continental Powers at the same time; secondly, to engage the latter first, disarming England by conciliation, if not obtaining her help by bribes. When we consider with what triumphant success he humbled Germany and Russia between 1805 and 1807, and that he held the German Powers successfully in submission till 1812, and then recollect that during all this time he was also waging war with England, the question suggests itself, What might he not have done if only he had remained at peace with England? But for England, the Peninsula would not have pressed upon him with such a fatal weight. But for England, the avenging coalition formed in 1813 would have wanted both money and credit — would have wanted the cement that held it together. And a second question arises: For what purpose did he maintain these unceasing hostilities with England, hostilities 'nullos habitura triumphos'? In this war no victories were won or could be won; after 1805 it was but a monotonous blockade, maintained by England until the time came when England could take the offensive in the Peninsula, but no offensive was possible on the side of France. As soon as this question is asked, we remark another fact, which is of the first importance, viz. that the war with England began in 1803, though peace had been signed only the year before, and that it began with marks of great passion on the side of Bonaparte, whereas the war with the Continental Powers was still delayed for two years, and then had all the appearance of being forced on, not by Bonaparte, but by the other Powers. He did not turn his armies in the direction of Germany till he had become convinced of the impossibility of invading England, and even then he only marched to repel a threatened invasion.

It appears, then, that when he broke the peace of Amiens in 1803, he cannot at least have had in view such a continental empire as he actually founded. He was thinking of something not less great, but of something different, viz. the conquest or humiliation of the British Empire. He did not suppose that he should fail in the invasion of England, and suddenly substitute for it an invasion of Germany; he anticipated success in his first plan.

But he was alive from the outset to the extreme difficulty of the invasion. Accordingly he held in reserve, as we learn from a paper of Talleyrand, written just before the rupture of 1803, an alternative plan. 'England,' writes Talleyrand, 'may compel France to conquer Europe.' It is characteristic of Napoleon throughout his career, that he keeps two plans in his head at once, and is at all times ready, if one fails, to fall back upon the other. 'I always,' he said, 'work out my problem in two ways.'

It thus appears that the actual Napoleonic Empire, as it was founded between 1805 and 1807, was not a work deliberately designed by Napoleon. It was his *pis aller*. His original plan had been to engage England singly, and to crush her. The fall of the British Empire was to take place in the years 1803 and 1804. This was Napoleon's object.

This plan failed. The English naval power proved too great, and Pitt, recalled to office, brought into existence a new Continental coalition. Thereupon Napoleon put into execution his alternative plan. Instead of conquering England directly, he would conquer the Continent, and by that means England. As Talleyrand foresaw, the first part of this plan proved not difficult to execute. He did conquer the Continent, and he marshalled all its forces against England. The enterprise was colossal, and the duel between a confederated Europe and the World-Empire of England was an unparalleled spectacle. But difficulties arose which had been but imperfectly foreseen. The confederacy, being held together by force, was but half efficient; when required to sacrifice the English trade, it became mutinous; gradually the idea of conquering England by means of a European confederacy showed itself to be — like that earlier conception of the same mind, a revolution of the East effected through a fusion of Mohammedanism with French Deism — merely a dazzling chimera.

Thus viewed, Napoleon appears not as a mere ambitious sovereign, aiming at universal empire, but as having a more definite plan.

His end is the defeat of England; what we call his universal empire is but a means to it.

He sees but one enemy, England; he engages England alone, but England calls the Continent to her aid. He masters the Continent, and turns its resources against England. Then again, after Tilsit, he has but one enemy, England. But his monstrous design requires monstrous expedients.

As he has to deal with a colonial and naval Power, he finds it necessary to control all the maritime states of Europe. Hence the seizure of Spain and Portugal, which brought him ships and colonies; hence the annexation of Holland and the Hanseatic towns. So much violence provoked mutiny. The rising of Germany in 1809 he was able to suppress; but a little later the Czar placed himself at the head of the insurrection of Europe. The mutiny of the Czar could only be suppressed by a prodigious effort, and in this effort Napoleon failed.

The point to be especially noted is that in this Russian war, as in all the violent annexations which mark the years between the Russian war and the Treaty of Tilsit, the ground openly avowed is always the commercial system and the war with England. In truth, what we call the universal empire of Napoleon would be more appropriately called the universal coalition against England. The territory actually ruled by Napoleon and his family by no means amounted to a universal empire; and Prussia, Austria, and Russia always remained outside it; but the coalition against England included these Powers too, and even in some sense the United States.

§ 2. *Origin of the Plan.*

Regarded so, Napoleon's plan, though, as the event proved, unsound, appears intelligible — vitiated only, as a Napoleonic plan might naturally be, by extravagance and exaggeration. But this view suggests the further question, Why was Napoleon so bent upon compassing the fall of the British Empire? The answer to this question is simple and natural, but shows perhaps that the workings of Napoleon's mind were more like those of an ordinary statesman than we are apt to think.

After his return from Italy at the end of 1797 he had been appointed, as we have seen, general of the 'army of England.' It was at first expected that in 1798 he would invade

England, but after due consideration he rejected this plan, and substituted for it an invasion of Egypt. This enterprise was directed ostensibly and in part, though only in part, really against England; but England opposed it with a vigor which she has seldom displayed. The heroism of Nelson has always been duly recognized, but the immense greatness of his work seems to have been generally overlooked. At Aboukir he reconquered, as it were, the Mediterranean for England. He dissolved, at a blow, all Napoleon's dreams of colonization and Oriental conquest. Soon afterwards he broke up the Armed Neutrality. Abercrombie crowned the work of Nelson in Egypt, and France had really no resource but to conclude peace. As Ranke says, 'the man of the century had entirely failed. . . . Nothing remained for the First Consul but to recognize the maritime predominance of England.' At the very height of her greatness France had suffered a complete naval defeat at the hands of England.

No further explanation surely is needed of the persistent hostility with which Napoleon henceforth pursued England. The all-powerful master of France had not only been beaten, had not only been forced to yield Egypt, but soon after the treaty had been concluded, he saw also that England was likely to keep Malta. It was too much for him that his darling enterprise should end not even in simple nothing, but in delivering over to the enemy one of the strongest positions in the world. The rupture of the peace of Amiens was not so much as it seems a deliberate new beginning in Napoleon's life. It was but the recommencement of a war which had never really ceased, the retractation at the last moment of a step which Napoleon found after all intolerable. And, war being once recommenced, it was not likely that he would put up with failure. Yet he found all his maritime plans in 1803 and 1804 fail. In 1805 England met him with a European coalition, and he found himself drawn into the wild crusade above described, into the attempt to conquer England by conquering Europe.

It appears, then, that Napoleon formed no deliberate plan of universal empire, but in the first instance, merely took up the foreign policy of the Governments that had preceded him. He waged war with England merely because they had done so ever since 1793; he conducted the war with passionate and at last with insane persistency, merely because he could not conquer this enemy as he had conquered others, because he had naval defeats to wipe out; because it was intolerable to him, and not even safe, to put up with failure. But his military resources being as enormous as his naval resources were insufficient, and the new coalition affording him an opportunity of striking England by striking Austria and Russia, the war with England converted itself insensibly into a war with the allies of England, and Napoleon consoled himself for not being able to enter London by entering Vienna, Berlin, and Moscow. In all this there was nothing really new except the immense magnitude of the military operations.

If we trace the foreign policy of France from the beginning of the eighteenth century, we find, first, a naval and colonial rivalry with England, which grows steadily more intense; secondly, a constant disposition to interfere and play the ascendant power in Germany; thirdly, a proneness to spoil either game by trying to play both at once. The war with England, begun by Napoleon in 1803, was the fifth which France had undertaken in a period of sixty years. A generation earlier, Frederick the Great had spoken with impatience of the interminable quarrel of England and France,

which allowed no peace to Europe. But both in
the War of the Austrian Succession and in the
Seven Years' War, the rivalry had blended itself
in a most confusing manner with other quarrels
which France made for herself in Germany. This
confusion had always proved most disastrous to
France, and Chatham had been able, as he said,
to conquer Canada in Germany. Nevertheless,
the first step taken by the Convention was to
repeat the old blunder by declaring war with
England at the very moment when the French republic was struggling for life against the Continental Powers. If Napoleon had been able, as
we are apt to think, to look down upon French
politics from a superior height, if he had thought
of inventing a new policy of his own, he would
probably have begun by correcting this error, and
would either have made peace with England, or,
while he went to war with England, would have
taken pains to propitiate the Continental Powers.
But, like most statesmen, he was fettered by the
past, and his career was spoiled in the end by the
false policy which he inherited from the eighteenth
century, and which he practised on an exaggerated scale. He adopts the old methods of the
eighteenth century, the armed neutrality and the
occupation of Hanover; by placing a brother on

the throne of Spain he revives the family compact. But his exceptional position enables him to go beyond the eighteenth century, and to form against the so-called tyrant of the seas a stronger coalition than she had formed against the ascendency of Louis XIV. But this coalition is formed by force, and is a greater tyranny than that against which it is directed. Accordingly in the moment of need it passes over to the English side, and France is once more found to have overreached herself by undertaking a war with England and a war with the Continent at the same time.

§ 3. *Execution of the Plan.*

It appears, then, that the special and peculiar work of Napoleon is that colossal attempt to conquer England by conquering Europe. Another general, a Moreau, if he had been raised to supreme power at Brumaire, would in like manner have found himself involved in war with England, would have met with the same difficulties, would have been equally reluctant to part with Malta, possibly would have felt himself impelled to break the peace of Amiens. But his ideas and his resolutions would have been less extreme; he would have been less impatient of failure. When he became clearly aware of England's naval superiority, he would have made peace, and contented himself with undermining it gradually. For Napoleon this does not suffice; he presses the war against England's allies, as though his object was the subjugation of the Continent. And yet his power did not increase much after 1803, when his ascendency, alike in Italy, Spain, and Germany, was unbounded, and, wisely handled, might have been raised much higher. He did but substitute for this an invidious tyranny, which could be maintained only by an unintermitted effort and uninterrupted good fortune. A Moreau, such as we have described him, might even have been more powerful than Napoleon. Had he witnessed the new coalition, he would have felt it as a failure of his policy that the wild times before Brumaire should be reappearing. He too, probably, would have won considerable successes against the German Powers, but he would not have ventured upon the enormous hazards of the Austerlitz campaign. The idea of conquering England by conquering Europe would have struck him as insane; he would have said, untruly, that it was impossible of execution, and more reasonably, that it was a reckless adventure. Accordingly, France would have had no Austerlitz, no Jena, no Friedland to boast of, and her ruler would not have distributed crowns among his brothers, or married an archduchess. But he might without great difficulty have continued for many years to be incomparably the greatest sovereign in Europe, and without actually entering Vienna he might have entirely eclipsed Austria within the empire, and have gathered the smaller German states round him in a Confederation of the Rhine.

For the ruler personally such a career would have been brilliant enough. Had he been Moreau, he would perhaps have imitated Washington, and handed the Presidency over to another after a limited term. But if we suppose him less disinterested, he might, like Napoleon, have established an hereditary throne. Along with Jacobinism, France might have given up all that belonged to the Second Revolution, and have returned to the Liberal Monarchy of 1791, correcting only the great mistake of that constitution, which consisted in giving too little power to the executive. With such a monarchy Europe would have been disposed to live at peace. It would have suited France, in which monarchism had struck far deeper roots than could be eradicated in a few years of republican government. The Bourbons would have been forgotten, the monarchical party of France would have transferred its allegiance, and, preserved from that double schism which afterwards ruined it, would perhaps have continued to this day to form the vast majority of the nation. That nation would include at least Belgium, the left bank of the Rhine, Savoy, and Nice.

We see, then, precisely how history was modified by the exceptional character of Napoleon. He neither made peace with England, nor concentrated his force upon her, carefully conciliating the Continental Powers, nor endeavored by diplomacy to form a European coalition against her, but plunged into the enterprise of forcing the Continent by arms into a confederacy against her. Yet he had himself, in 1800, shown the possibility of reviving by negotiation the Armed Neutrality; nor would it have been difficult for him, by moderate conduct in 1804 and 1805, to avert at least the third coalition.

Evidently no political instrument can be less trustworthy than a confederacy held together by force. The defection, first of Spain, then of Prussia, then of Austria, could cause no surprise. And apparently it had been open to Napoleon in 1803 to create a voluntary confederacy, which would have reduced England to a great extremity without endangering Napoleon's power. Yet, not only at the outset, but at every stage of his progress, he seems deliberately to prefer forced alliances, the result of a war, to any free combination of interests. He had Prussia as an ally, but preferred to have her as a subject; he was enthusiastically followed by Spain, but preferred to plunder and humiliate her; and he throws away his alliance with Russia, choosing deliberately to recover it at the head of 600,000 men.

§ 4. *Was he successful?*

'Better in a battle than in a war' is the phrase which Livy applies to Hannibal. But the popular view regards only battles, and seems unable to embrace a whole war, still less a comprehensive political scheme in which even a war may be but an episode. Hence the prevalent notion of Napoleon as a kind of incarnation of success. In whatever way we conceive success, Napoleon missed it, and if the Cæsars and Alexanders may be called the gods of history, Napoleon is the Titan. If we ascribe to him a purely personal ambition, he would have been successful if he had established his dynasty in France. To any one who saw him about 1802, it must have seemed that such an object was easily within his reach, if only he could stoop to pick up a crown. He did stoop, he picked up the crown, but it dropped from his hands again. Everything favored this ambition, the profoundly monarchical disposition of the country, the total failure of the Jacobins on the one side, and of the Bourbons on the other, his own military achievements, which, as early as 1802, were unrivalled in modern history. The success with which, a generation later, his nephew traded on his mere name, is a measure of the mistakes which caused his own ruin and that of his son.

But let us suppose that he had higher views, that he thought of the greatness and well-being of France. What was the effect upon France of the specially Napoleonic work, of the attempt to conquer England by conquering Europe? As in the popular view the triumphant success which this enterprise had in its earlier stages, seems to conceal the total failure which it met with in the end, so it makes us utterly blind to the irretrievable disaster which it brought upon France. Much, it is true, has been said of the loss of life incurred, and indeed the statistics of the campaigns of 1812, 1813, 1814, 1815, are appalling. But the bloodshed fell upon several nations at once. What was peculiar to France was the loss of territory. And it was not merely the conquests made by

Napoleon that were lost. We may indeed hold that France suffered no real loss by the dissolution of the Confederation of the Rhine, or by the expulsion of her armies from Spain and Italy, that the fall of the Napoleonic Empire was to France but the removal of an unhealthy excrescence. But France lost more than this; she lost not merely the conquests of Napoleon, but those of the Revolution; and these stand on quite another footing. She had held Belgium for twenty years, and the left bank of the Rhine for nearly as long a time. None of the acquisitions made by France under the Bourbons seemed more solid and secure than these. They had cost France dear, and the loss of them had been felt as an almost incurable wound to Germany. But the transference had been effected, the struggle was over, the European system had adapted itself to the change. Other questions had arisen since. For a long time after the Treaty of Lunéville it was not thought likely that the result of the revolutionary war would be undone again, or that France could be forced back within her ancient limits.

To a Moreau or a Bernadotte it would probably have been an easy task to defend these acquisitions, for there was no discontent, no indignant outraged patriotism in the annexed territories, and how could Europe in cold blood tear them by main force from such a Power as France? Napoleon found the way to lose them.

When we speak of Napoleon as a great conqueror, do we consider that he not only lost all his conquests, but left the territory of France actually smaller than he found it when he became its ruler? Belgium was no part of his conquests; the left bank of the Rhine was an acquisition for which France thanked him only among others; and this splendid tract of territory, which seemed as safely incorporated with France as Burgundy, was lost by Napoleon.

The title 'Mehrer des Reichs' was deserved by several Bourbon princes. Henry II. won the three bishoprics, Alsace and Franche Comté are the trophies of Louis XIV., Lorraine and Corsica those of Louis XV. The struggle by which the First Republic had deserved the same title, and of which Belgium and the Left Bank were the trophies, was grander than any of these. What is the trophy of Napoleon? Alone of all the modern rulers of France, he inflicted upon her a vast and irreparable loss of territory.

And yet not alone, for Alsace and Lorraine have gone since; but they too have been lost in his name, and by recurring to his system.

§ 5. *How far his Influence was Beneficial.*

The beneficial consequences which may be traced to Napoleon's career fall into two principal classes: (1) those caused not by him, but by resistance to him; (2) those caused by him as the child of his age or the representative of the Revolution.

(1.) It is said, Did not he carry a refreshing, regenerating influence wherever he appeared at the head of his armies? Do not several European states date their modern period of progress and regeneration from a Napoleonic invasion? This is true at least of Prussia, Russia, and Spain; but in what sense is it true? In the same sense in which the greatness of ancient Greece is to be traced to the invasion of Xerxes. A pressing danger, the necessity of a great national rally, if it is followed by victory, is the most beneficial thing that can happen to a state. In Prussia the reform commenced by Stein and Scharnhorst and the victories of the war of liberation which followed, in Russia and Spain the heroic resistance, had the effect of inspiring these nations as nothing had done before. But as the Greeks did not honor Xerxes for the great impulse they had received from the efforts which caused his defeat, so we ought to consider that it was not Napoleon, but resistance to Napoleon, which had such a bracing effect upon Europe. Did he intend to rouse national spirit? What he ultimately intended it is indeed difficult to say. Possibly he calculated that the military tyranny which he exercised would not be long needed, and that it would cease as a matter of course, when the fall of England should be accomplished. But he certainly did not intend to rouse in Germany and Italy a political consciousness leading to national unity and liberty; still less did he intend to create that rebellion in Spain which was fatal to his empire. He intended in these cases the opposite result, as we see by the great impulse which he gave to despotism in the middle states of Germany, and by the pains he took to prevent his Russian expedition from leading to a restoration of Poland. Had he been successful — that is, had English influence been destroyed and English liberties been overthrown, had Prussia been reduced to a mere electorate, and Piedmont to a French province, had the system of French imperialism been consolidated in Germany, Italy, and Spain, — all the movements which have since made the life and animated the history of this century would have been precluded. Napoleon's own direct influence tended to ruin and to the stagnation of imperialism, and was only beneficial in backward countries such as Spain and

Italy; the regenerating influence of that age is the spirit of resistance to Napoleon. It was the great Anti-Napoleonic Revolution of Europe which, by arming the peoples against tyranny, laid the foundation of European liberty.

(2.) It is however true that he professed, in a vague manner, to be the champion of the liberal principles of the First Revolution, that is, of civil equality, religious toleration, and enlightened legislation. And it is possible to show that liberal reforms of this kind were introduced by his government in the Rhine provinces, in Westphalia, and in Italy. Naturally the expansion of France which followed the Revolution had many such beneficial consequences. But that expansion was not specifically his work. It began before him; it would have proceeded almost as far without him. Had Moreau reigned instead of Bonaparte, a similar influence would have flowed from liberal France upon the neighboring states; it would have flowed more constantly and more uniformly, and it would have been followed by no similar reaction. Such liberal reforms are not specifically Napoleonic; they belong to the movement which bore him along, not to that which he himself originated.

The same remark applies to his domestic reforms. When he did only what Moreau or Bernadotte would have done in his place, he often did what was good in itself, and he did it with remarkable energy. Thus it fell to him, wielding the first strong government that had been seen since the destruction of ancient France, to found a whole system of national institutions, Army, Church, University, Bank, Local Government, Code. Modern France dates from the Consulate. And it may be possible to show that in some parts of the new system his own mind has left its stamp, and also that no ruler less energetic would have met the needs of the time so fully. Still in the main this work was done by committees of experts, and it was done at that time and at no other, not because Napoleon was specially enlightened, but because the country found itself at last at peace and almost without institutions. A Moreau would have done perhaps not so much, but he must have done a similar work; and it is easy to show that, being disinterested, he might have avoided great legislative errors, into which Napoleon was led by his rapacity of power.

A similar remark may be applied to that great work of discipline, for which he often receives credit. It is said that his firm will, vigilant eye, and indefatigable energy presiding for years over every department of administration, gave an impulse to the public service and a discipline to officials, which, passing afterwards into a tradition of conscientious work, has upheld the French state ever since. No doubt the contrast is great between the stern martial energy of the Napoleonic generation and the effeminacy of the age of Pompadour. But here, again, the reform had been begun and was even far advanced when Napoleon appeared. It had been set on foot by the Convention: Marceau, Kléber, Hoche, in the army, Carnot in the Government, had set great examples, which an organized imperialism could not but emulate; and what Bonaparte did in this respect would have been done by a Moreau, with less energy no doubt, but with a purer spirit.

§ 6. *Napoleon judged by his Plan.*

When we compare Napoleon's way of thinking with that of other rulers of the same class, even the most ambitious, we seem to see a difference. Louis XIV. and Frederick are thought ambitious, but they were scarcely ambitious in the same sense as Napoleon. Their course was unscrupulous and lawless, but in most cases they aimed at acquisitions which were really important, nay, often seemed indispensably necessary to the country.

Thus by the partition of Poland Frederick at once rescued Prussia from a position of extreme difficulty, and acquired a province which seemed almost indispensable for the compactness of the kingdom. Louis XIV. also had for the most part a serious public object in view. To fortify France on the side where she was weakest, to complete the incorporation of Alsace, acquired during his minority, were objects so important that we may suppose many of his aggressions to have seemed to him justifiable on the ground of necessary self-defence. The feverish impatience with which the Emperor Joseph presses his wild schemes of annexation, is certainly to be explained by the extreme and dangerous want of compactness which he found in the Austrian territory. Napoleon, in adopting the unscrupulous maxims of the eighteenth century school of rulers, applies them not only on a scale which would have appalled the most cynical of these, but also in cases which they did not contemplate. They pleaded self-defence and public necessity for their annexations. The plea was insufficient, but for the most part it was urged in sincerity. The same excuse of necessity and self-defence might be offered for the lawless conduct of the French Government in the first years of the revolutionary war. The country was at one time in extreme danger, and in addition the revolutionists sincerely believed that humanity itself was interested in their success. We may allow to Napoleon himself, so long as he was Bonaparte, the benefit of this excuse.

But it cannot be alleged for the wars of the properly Napoleonic period, that is, the wars after 1803. France was now in no danger, and could urge no plea of necessity or self-defence. Her territory was greatly enlarged, and it was compact. When Napoleon now continued to practise the doctrine of Frederick and Joseph, he applied it to a state of things for which it had never been intended. His language was less cynical than Frederick's, because it was less frank; but his conduct was far more immoral. Frederick's ambition is sincerely for the state; it is for the state he sins; and he seeks for the state real, unquestionable, solid advantages. But for a state like France, at the height of prosperity and glory, to adopt in an ordinary colonial and maritime war against England the desperate maxims by which Frederick and Joseph had sought to found solid and defensible states in the midst of the confusion of Germany — this was not to follow a bad precedent, but to pervert a bad precedent into something infinitely worse. It was portentous and unique in the Napoleonic policy, that, while it far surpassed that of Frederick in cynicism and waste of human life, it had no definable object; for who could say what shape Europe would take, or how it would be governed, when the maritime tyranny of England should once for all be overthrown?

Moreover, while he exaggerates the bad maxims of the past age, he shows no sympathy for the better maxims which his own age was substituting for them. The Machiavelism of the eighteenth century marked the dissolution of the old system. What better system was to arise? Frederick and Joseph could not be expected to know, but Napoleon might have known. His own unrivalled glory came from the leadership of a living nationality; he better than any man of his time might have foreseen that the nineteenth century would make Germany, Russia, Italy, Spain, *organic*, as France had been made organic by her revolution. This development would create a new European system, in which no doubt wars would still have a place and armies become larger than ever, yet far nobler than the family system of the seventeenth century or the international anarchy of the eighteenth. I have said that Napoleon did not originate the lawlessness he practised, that he only reflected the morality of his age; unfortunately he reflected only one part of it, and presented a rugged, dull surface to the better part. He had assimilated all that Frederick could teach, but the generous maxims of the first French Revolution had made no impression on him. And yet he, a pupil of Paoli, a native of that Corsica which had been to Rousseau what Greece was later to Byron —so that he had exclaimed, 'I have a kind of presentiment that this little island will astonish Europe'— should have entered more than any of his contemporaries into all that is expressed by the word 'nationality.' It was indeed expected of him; the primitive type of heroism, founded on devotion to the fatherland, seemed embodied in the Corsican soldier with his classical face. It is therefore a strikingly individual trait that he altogether disappoints these expectations. As in Corsica itself he turned against Paoli, so in Europe he will know nothing of the principle of nationality. He goes all lengths in warring against it, so that at last he becomes absolutely identified with the tyranny against which 'Plutarch's men' fight. It is as if Tell should transform himself into Gessler, or Leonidas into Xerxes. And no hereditary tyrant, warring on national independence in mere invincible ignorance of its nature, was ever more ruthless and relentless than this tyrant, who had been bred in an atmosphere of national ideas. The oppressor of Tyrol and Spain is actually the same man who only twenty years earlier had written the 'Letters on Corsica.'

But, forsooth, everything must yield to the paramount necessity of bringing to an end the maritime tyranny of England. We can enter into the frenzy of the ruler who, while he meets with no resistance elsewhere, finds himself steadily thwarted in the one direction in which from the beginning he had resolved to move. Germany, and Spain, and Russia felt the impatient force, which could not find an escape at Brest and Rochefort. And as he grew accustomed year after year to war on a large scale, it became perhaps more and more an object in itself. The character, which had always been remarked for its lonely pride and egoism, became, thus indulged on the one side and thwarted on the other, cynically unlike that of other men — inhuman. The former generation had trembled at the hard cynicism of Frederick, but human life was now wasted on a vastly greater scale, liberty more ruthlessly repressed, public law more contemptuously outraged, by one who sprang from the people. Frederick had pursued intelligible objects, but Napoleon's objects were scarcely definable. At last, when he sacrificed half a million of men in Russia to his crotchet of a commercial system, he seemed to pass out of the pale of civilized humanity, and to rank himself with Attila. The comparison was superficial; but had Napoleon, or had Attila, the better right to complain of it? The barbarian followed the maxims of his age and people, but we can only look with stupefaction on the Russian expedition. For we remember that this most monstrous of human sacrifices was performed by the person who twenty years earlier was pronounced ' a man of sensibility,' when he discussed in the style of Rousseau 'what sentiments it is important to inculcate upon human beings for their happiness.'

Where it is possible, the best way to estimate the moral character of a man is to consider the general purpose and drift of his life. Particular acts usually admit of palliation or excuse ; in a time so revolutionary as that in which Napoleon lived, almost every act may be plausibly defended on the plea of an exceptional necessity. No one has ever accused Napoleon of purely wanton crimes, such crimes as spring from an unhealthy nature. His crimes are for the most part acts of lawless violence, done openly, avowed, and justified by the reason of state. The language he uniformly held shows that he had adopted early, and with great decision, the maxim so current in the revolutionary age, that as long as the public good is our object, almost every act is permissible; or, as Mirabeau was fond of repeating, 'La petite morale est ennemie de la grande.' We may say that he elects to be tried by the standard of Frederick the Great. He does not profess to observe the morality of ordinary men; as Frederick frankly maintains that for the public good treaties may be broken, so Napoleon will break any engagement and violate any law for the public good.

This principle is terrible; nevertheless it is a principle. Those who sincerely adhere to it will subject themselves to a certain restraint, will recognize certain acts to be criminal, and certain other acts to be obligatory. For Frederick himself, perhaps, the principle had really its positive as well as its negative side. The public good was to him perhaps no mere pretext, no mere synonyme for his own interest. In his career, as we see the negative working of the principle in such particular acts as the invasion of Silesia and the partition of Poland, so we see the positive working of it in the general tendency of the whole. We see that at the beginning of his reign the Prussian state labored under great disadvantages, which exposed it to great dangers. We see that it is to remove these disadvantages that Frederick devotes his life and commits his crimes. When he speaks of the public good he is serious, and we may, perhaps, acquit him on the whole of a purely selfish ambition. Hence he is remembered with gratitude by the Germany of the present day.

The attempt has been made here to apply the same method to Napoleon. It is the only method which is sufficiently compendious to be admissible in a work of this kind, and it is perhaps in itself the most satisfactory. All his lawless deeds were regarded by him as means to an end, justified by the goodness of the end. He was full of the idea that he had to deal with a revolutionary age, to which ordinary maxims are inapplicable. 'You understand nothing of revolutions,' was his contemptuous comment, when some one related how he had yielded to a moral scruple at some crisis of French affairs. If this was his view, what can be gained by nicely sifting the evidence on which the special charges against him rest? 'Such men as I,' he said, 'do not commit crimes;' that is, they do what is necessary, and what is necessary is right.

But Napoleon, like Frederick, had so much freedom and power that we are able to discover what general objects he has in view. We are able to apply to him the tests he himself accepts.

From about the middle of the period of the Consulate he begins to be as free from all pledges and all responsibility as Frederick had been, and therefore from this date onward he reveals his own personal aims, whereas earlier he had been but an instrument of the aims of the French Revolution.

In the former period, therefore, we see the man such as circumstances made him. He is the incarnation of the vitality of a great people, made organic for the first time. They have the instinct of subordination, formed in the time of despotism, and along with it the new feeling of life. Of such a nation he becomes the heroic king, in order to vindicate it and subdue its enemies. This period comes to an end in the Consulate, when Bonaparte accomplishes the pacification of the world.

In the latter period we see the man such as he is in himself. He now no longer executes a commission derived from others, but forms his own plans. In the execution of them he is, like Frederick, unscrupulous. Both at home and abroad he makes slight account of engagements; like Frederick, too, he is hard and careless of human life. Moreover, as his power is far greater, his reckless violence oppresses mankind far more than Frederick's had done. The carnage and horror of the Seven Years' War are utterly eclipsed on the fields of Borodino and Leipzig, and in the retreat from Moscow. And, still further, he is himself the prime mover in the incessant wars of this period; whereas Frederick, after the invasion of Silesia, had remained for the most part on the defensive. But, like Frederick, he justifies his course by the plea of the public good.

He pushes this wild morality to the utmost extreme. For it is scarcely possible to imagine any reform or improvement in human affairs so great as to compensate for all that Napoleon inflicted on mankind — for France decimated, for Russia invaded, for Spain made for five years the scene of a barbarous civil war, for Germany trampled under foot, for England blockaded, for a whole generation sacrificed to war. Still, in estimating Napoleon's character, the essential question is, Had he really the public good in view? Had he some object which, if it could be attained, might conceivably seem to him worth so many sacrifices, and which he might conceivably hope to attain by means of them? If he had, we may regard his career as in a certain sense magnanimous, if also wayward, and even monstrous: we may regard him as a great spirit laboring under a terrible but still sublime hallucination.

Our conclusion is that he had neither any such

grand conception, nor yet, on the other hand, the bare desire for personal glory. He pursued simply the ordinary objects of the French Foreign Office, and only failure and the impatience caused by failure led him to strain in such an unheard-of manner the enormous resources of his empire. His aim was to fight out the great quarrel with England which had occupied France throughout the eighteenth century, to avenge and repair the losses France had suffered in Canada and India, and on all the seas. This was what he promised to France; and being unable to accomplish his object by a direct attack, he forced all Europe into the war, 'conquering Europe into order to conquer England,' and offering nothing to Europe in return but the old points of the Armed Neutrality.

This is what he promised; and what he promised he failed to perform, causing France to lose in the attempt all the dear-bought conquests of the Revolution.

When we review the career of Frederick the Great, we cannot refrain, however severely we may judge his crimes, from reflecting that after all his monument is modern Germany. That solid structure remains to honor the workman who did so much to build it. It is, in the main, just such a structure as Frederick would have desired to see, as he intended to found.

For Napoleon, too, it may be said that modern France, in its internal constitution, is his monument. Its institutions are in the main the work of his reign. But this is the monument of that earlier Napoleon who was the child of his age.

The Napoleon who was *himself*, who executed his iron plans with almost unlimited power, has no monument. All that he built, at such a cost of blood and tears, was swept away before he himself ended his short life.

University Press: John Wilson and Son, Cambridge.

J. R. SEELEY'S WRITINGS.

ECCE HOMO. A Survey of the Life and Work of Jesus Christ. 16mo. Price $1.00.

"It will do a service among a very large class of readers, such as are assigned to hardly more than two or three volumes in a century." — *Rev. George E Ellis.*

"This remarkable book is one of those which permanently influence public opinion. The author has a right to claim deference from those who think deepest and know most, when he pleads before them that not philosophy can save and reclaim the world, but faith in a divine person who is worthy of it, allegiance to a divine society which he founded, and union of hearts in the object for which he created it." — *The Guardian.*

"By general consent, the most remarkable book of recent years." — *Christian Examiner.*

ROMAN IMPERIALISM, and other Lectures and Essays. 16mo. Price $1.50.

CONTENTS: Roman Imperialism. I. The Great Roman Revolution; II. The Proximate Cause of the Fall of the Roman Empire. — Milton's Political Opinions. — Milton's Poetry. — Elementary Principles in Art. — Liberal Education in Universities. — English in Schools. — The Church as a Teacher of Morality. — The Teaching of Politics, an Inaugural Lecture, delivered at Cambridge.

"The author of 'Ecce Homo' has been pronounced the typical writer of the present time. Those who have read his former work — and who has not? — will give this a cordial welcome. The essays entitled 'Liberal Education in Universities,' 'English in Schools,' and 'The Teaching of Politics,' challenge the attention of educators; while 'The Church as a Teacher of Morality' will excite some of the fierce criticism that followed the publication of 'Ecce Homo.'" — *St. Louis Journal of Education.*

NATURAL RELIGION. With a new Explanatory Preface. 16mo. Price $1.25.

"The author of 'Ecce Homo' has now spoken again with the view of showing Christ as the creator of modern theology and religion, or rather of showing how far the republic of God, as set up in the world through the agency of Jesus Christ, fulfils its functions in the last quarter of the nineteenth century. The bold hand that stripped from the name of Christ the thousand superstitions that surrounded him, here deals with Christianity as he then dealt with its originator; and the same strong criticism, the same fearless assertion of fundamental principles, the same comprehensiveness of view, the same desire to explain by natural what has so often been rem inded to supernatural forces, the same grasp of the ethical convictions of men, appears in 'Natural Religion' that startled thinking people in the pages of 'Ecce Homo.'" — *Sunday Herald.*

THE EXPANSION OF ENGLAND. Crown 8vo. Price $1.75.

"Those who take even the slightest interest in historical reading cannot fail to be absorbed and delighted by Professor Seeley's book." — *Washington Herald.*

"The 'Expansion of England,' by J. R. Seeley, M.A., consists of two courses of lectures delivered by the author at Cambridge University, where he is Regius Professor of Modern History. It is a brilliant volume, charming in style, and of the highest interest in the method chosen by the author for the marshalling and development of his subject. There are eight lectures in all, and they show, with rare skill in the management and condensation of a vast amount of material, how and why England, from small beginnings, had reached her present position, and left the rest of Europe behind her in political and commercial progress." — *Saturday Evening Gazette.*

Sold by all Booksellers. Mailed, post-paid, by the Publishers,

ROBERTS BROTHERS, BOSTON.

IMPORTANT HISTORICAL WORK BY THE AUTHOR
OF "ECCE HOMO."

Just ready, 2 Vols., 8vo, with Portrait and Maps, price $7.50.

LIFE AND TIMES OF STEIN;
OR,
Germany and Prussia in the Napoleonic Age.
BY J. R. SEELEY, M.A.,
Regius Professor of Modern History in the University of Cambridge, Eng.

This book is drawn almost entirely from German sources which neither English nor French writers have yet explored, and it describes events which form the beginning of the modern history of Prussia, and others which are very important in the history of Europe.

The author has kept students of history constantly in view. It is a favorite opinion of his that recent history ought to be introduced into education, and this book is intended to be such as can be introduced into universities and the higher forms of schools.

From the Hartford Courant.

"The 'Life and Times of Stein,' by Professor Seeley of Oxford, author of 'Ecce Homo,' is a work of great importance to students of political history. The subject of it, we may remark by the way, is honored in Berlin by what is probably the finest statue made in modern times. And this consummate work of art is only a fit recognition of the pre-eminent service that Baron Von Stein rendered to Prussia. It is scarcely too much to say that Stein is the creator of modern Prussia, and that but for him the successful career of Prince Bismarck, the architect of German unity, would have been impossible."

From the London Athenæum.

"In a notice of this kind scant justice can be done to a work like the one before us; no short *résumé* can give even the most meagre notion of the contents of these volumes, which contain no page that is superfluous, and none that is uninteresting. Every day the interest attaching to the present political condition of Germany increases; every day we see more and more clearly the outlines of the great constitutional struggles, possibly of the revolution, that must surely soon come about. To understand the Germany of to-day, one must study the Germany of many yesterdays; and now that study has been made easy by this work, to which no one can hesitate to assign a very high place among those recent histories which have aimed at original research."

From the London Saturday Review.

"Mr. Seeley, the Regius Professor of Modern History at Cambridge, has made a valuable contribution to English knowledge of German history and German politics in a very elaborate sketch of the life and times of Stein. It is impossible to understand the present history of Germany without a previous acquaintance with the history of Germany, external and internal, in the Napoleonic era, with the labors of Stein and Hardenberg, and the preparations for Prussian strength and Prussian ascendancy. This field of historical research, so rich in instruction, was almost entirely untouched by English writers; and Mr. Seeley may be congratulated on having found a sphere for his labors which thoroughly deserved the patient industry, the exhaustive inquiry, and the discriminating impartiality with which he has approached his task."

Every library of any importance throughout the States should possess this important work. Sold everywhere. Mailed, postpaid, by the publishers,

ROBERTS BROTHERS, BOSTON.

www.ingramcontent.com/pod-product-compliance
Lightning Source LLC
Chambersburg PA
CBHW030744230426
43667CB00007B/836